Mr Steven Price
PO Box 52
Sequim, WA 98382

INTRODUCING
Kant

Christopher Kul-Want • Andrzej Klimowski

Edited by Richard Appignanesi

Icon Books UK　Totem Books USA

This edition published in the UK in 2005 by Icon Books Ltd., The Old Dairy, Brook Road, Thriplow, Cambridge SG8 7RG email: info@iconbooks.co.uk www.introducingbooks.com

Sold in the UK, Europe, South Africa and Asia by Faber and Faber Ltd., 3 Queen Square, London WC1N 3AU or their agents

Distributed in the UK, Europe, South Africa and Asia by TBS Ltd., TBS Distribution Centre, Colchester Road, Frating Green, Colchester CO7 7DW

This edition published in Australia in 2005 by Allen & Unwin Pty. Ltd., PO Box 8500, 83 Alexander Street, Crows Nest, NSW 2065

Previously published in the UK and Australia in 1996 under the title *Kant for Beginners* and in 1999 as *Introducing Kant*

Reprinted 2001, 2003, 2005, 2006

This edition published in the USA in 2005 by Totem Books Inquiries to Icon Books Ltd., The Old Dairy, Brook Road, Thriplow, Cambridge SG8 7RG, UK

Distributed to the trade in the USA by National Book Network Inc., 4720 Boston Way, Lanham, Maryland 20706

Distributed in Canada by Penguin Books Canada, 90 Eglinton Avenue East, Suite 700, Toronto, Ontario M4P 2YE

ISBN-10: 1-84046-664-2
ISBN-13: 978-1840466-64-5

Text copyright © 1996 Christopher Kul-Want
Illustrations copyright © 1996 Andrzej Klimowski

The author and artist have asserted their moral rights.

Originating editor: Richard Appignanesi

Printed and bound in Singapore
by Tien Wah Press

Situated at the threshold of modern thought, Kant's philosophy is marked by scepticism and a loss of faith in both religion and metaphysics. His writings are remarkable for the way in which they systematically refute any claim to know what the truth is, or where it lies.

If we say, 'There is no God', there is not the least contradiction in such a judgement

Yet, in the face of this overwhelming demolition of traditional beliefs, Kant's philosophy develops a new and profound sense of affirmation. It affirms the *limits* of human knowledge and the creative possibilities resulting from an acknowledgement of these limits. In place of superstition and dogma, Kant embraces change and human fallibility, recognizing these qualities to be the sources of pleasure. Such an outlook exceeds modernism's desire for order and progress and places Kant's thought within the turmoil of the postmodern.

Early Life

Immanuel Kant was born in the East Prussian city of Königsberg (now Kaliningrad) at 5 a.m., 22 April 1724. He was the fourth of nine children, three of whom died in infancy. His mother, Anna Regina, died when he was thirteen. Kant acknowledged a lasting debt to her love and instruction. She seems to have been the first to recognize his intellectual gifts.

It was she who decided to direct me toward an academic education.

His father, Johann Georg, was a harness-maker, and died when Kant was twenty-two. Kant spent his childhood in an artisanal suburb of Königsberg, growing up in an intensely **Pietist** milieu.

Königsberg was founded in the year of Kant's birth out of an amalgam of three large towns grouped around the River Pregel. Unlike other German cities of the period, Königsberg did not possess a closed urban élite consisting of patricians or local rural aristocracy.

It was the second largest city in Prussia and the most economically and culturally dynamic in Germany.

This allowed for a certain upward social mobility in the academic profession, owing to its particular economic and class structure.

Kant went to school at the Collegium Fridericianum, a private Pietist foundation, between 1732 and 1740, aided by the family pastor, Franz Albert Schütz, who was also a principal of the school.

We stress above all the felt power of God's grace to transform the believer's life through a conversion of "born again" experience.

In religious controversy, we urge that the aim should be to win over the heart of one's opponent rather than to gain intellectual victory.

I followed a rigorous and austere schooling in grammar and philology, accompanied by a régime of inflexible piety.

Pietism was founded in Germany by **Philipp Jakob Spener** (1635–1705). The Pietists regarded Christian faith not as a set of doctrinal propositions but as a living relationship with God.
For Pietism, the institution of the Lutheran church was considered less important than "the church invisible", whose membership in principle included the whole of humanity.

Despite Pietism's emphasis upon intuitive experience, its adherents laid great stress upon devotional exercises. A contemporary of Kant's at the Collegium Fridericianum, David Ruhnken, who later became teacher of philology at the University of Leiden, spoke of the "pedantic and gloomy discipline of fanatics" which dominated the organization of the school.

The curriculum of the institution was filled with uninterrupted prayers and periods of devotional exercises, with periods of edification, sermons and catechizing.

Theoretical classes were designed to insist upon the topics' relation to religious and theological questions.

Whilst Kant cherished the memory of the domestic Pietism of his parents and maintained respect for their traditional Pietist calm and serenity, he had nothing but scorn for the official version of Pietism encountered at school.

Partly under the influence of rational philosophy, he later became opposed in principle to religious ceremonies. In a letter of 1775 to J.C. Lavater he stated, "No confession of faith, no appeal to holy names nor any observance of religious ceremonies can help to gain salvation".

As rector of the University of Königsberg, he was always "indisposed" when his official participation in religious observances was required.

Kant's one inspiring teacher at the Fridericianum was the Latin master Heydenreich who introduced him to a life-long love of Latin literature. Of Heydenreich's other colleagues, Kant was later to comment . . .

Nevertheless, by the age of sixteen, Kant had fulfilled the state-imposed matriculation requirement of the local university.

Accounts of Kant during his early years as a student show him to be poor, although there are indications that he was supported financially by some of his fellow students in return for his help with their work!

The University of Königsberg was organized in the four traditional faculties, the three "higher faculties" of theology, law and medicine, and the fourth or "lower faculty" of philosophy. It is not known in which faculty Kant enrolled, but in spite of great poverty he did not pursue the qualification for a bureaucratic post in the Prussian administration.

> *I dedicated myself to the "lower faculty" of philosophy.*

For much of the 18th century, the lower faculty was the most dynamic and innovative in the university. Because its curriculum was not adapted to the demands of the university, the range of subjects covered by philosophy included physics and geography, ignored by the higher faculties, and even religion, jurisprudence and medicine, which were their protected domains.

The Enlightenment

Importantly, for Kant, the faculty of philosophy was in the best position to respond to the contemporary debates of the **Enlightenment**, in which developments in science were having their effect upon questions of metaphysics and religion.

Kant was introduced by his professor, **Martin Knutzen** (1714–51), to a wide range of material, including the ***Mathematical Principles of Natural Philosophy*** (or ***Principia***) by **Sir Isaac Newton** (1642–1727).

I defined a new science of dynamics and mechanics, concerned with the forces that hold the universe together.

Newton's principal contributions to science were to envisage interactions between particles other than solely through contact, and to give force a central role in the theory of matter, linking it directly with gravity.

PHILOSOPHIÆ
NATURALIS
PRINCIPIA
MATHEMATICA

Autore JS. NEWTON, Trin. Coll. Cantab. Soc. Mathefeos Professore Lucasiano, & Societatis Regalis Sodali.

IMPRIMATUR.
S. PEPYS, Reg. Soc. PRÆSES.
Julii 5. 1686:

LONDINI

Jussu Societatis Regiæ, ac Typis Josephi Streater. Prostant Venales apud Sam. Smith ad Insignia Principis Walliæ in Coemiterio D. Pauli, aliosque nonnullos Bibliopolas. Anno MDCLXXXVII.

Inevitably, Newton's theories reopened questions of **causality**. However, Newton himself countered the idea of a self-generating universe, by holding that gravitation was due to the direct action of God Himself.

Elsewhere in Europe, religion was under pressure from science. The Swedish botanist **Carolus Linnaeus** (1707–78) provided a new classification of plants built upon their sexuality (**Systema Naturae**, 1735).

I see nature as having a history far older than that suggested by Biblical chronology.

But I still saw nature as a harmonious and balanced system created by God.

Linnaeus' views were challenged by the naturalist **Georges-Louis Leclerc, Comte de Buffon** (1707–88) in his vast **Histoire Naturelle** (1749–67). Buffon argued that classifications were merely heuristic devices incapable of revealing the "real" structure of nature.

Buffon came close to the idea that species could change over time – a theory which foreshadows Darwin's evolutionism. These views, and his implicit support for the idea that man was intrinsically within the natural order, led to condemnations by the theology faculty of Paris in 1749.

Theories of Mind and Nature

Philosophers at this time regarded themselves as what we would now call "scientists". Our current distinction between philosophy and "science" did not yet exist. Even the "empirical" **David Hume** (1711–76) defined his moral philosophy as the "science of human nature". Hume saw his philosophy as analogous to the physical inquiries of Isaac Newton.

My branch of science is concerned with the secret springs and principles by which the human mind is actuated in its operations.

These philosophers, just prior to Kant, set the agenda for the classical "mind and body" (or "soul and body") problem, i.e., the study of **cognition**, which today is investigated as a "brain and mind" problem in experimental psychology.

Other contemporary philosophers, such as **Denis Diderot** (1713–84), co-editor of the monumental **_Encyclopédie_** (1751–72), applied themselves to the "nature" of life itself.

We produced a picture of "life" as the constitutive force of nature, an impulsion within living beings themselves to survive, to reproduce, and to obey the laws of their own existence.

Just as science unsettled transcendental views, so problems appeared in metaphysics itself!

"I have had the fate to be in love with metaphysics", wrote Kant in 1776, "although I can hardly flatter myself to have received favours from her". This unrequited love of metaphysics provided the leitmotif and underlying drama of Kant's whole career.

What is Metaphysics?

Metaphysics is a branch of philosophy that takes its name from the **Metaphysics** of **Aristotle** (384–322 B.C.), a number of his treatises or lecture courses, written at different times and brought together later by an unknown classical editor. He gave the title *Metaphysics* to this collection because the topics discussed follow the philosophy of nature (physics), as well as being concerned with reality as a whole (*meta* in Greek means above or beyond).

"There is a branch of knowledge that studies Being *qua* Being, and the attributes that belong to it in virtue of its own nature. Now this is not the same as any of the so-called special sciences, since none of these inquires universally about Being *qua* Being." (Aristotle, *Metaphysics*)

Aristotle's great predecessor **Plato** (c. 428–348 B.C.) had expressed a **dualistic** view of Being.

The concept of Being is equated with an eternal, transcendental world of unchanging Forms which exists in a hierarchical relation to the physical, corporeal world.

Plato's famous story of the cave in Book VII of **_The Republic_** (366 B.C.) illustrates his dualistic system. The story, told by Socrates, describes a group of prisoners who live in an underground cave, bound and chained so that they can only see straight ahead.

What they see on one of the walls of the cave are shadows of men "carrying all sorts of vessels, and statues and figures of animals made of

These men seem like marionette players who perform above a screen.

wood and stone and various materials". These men move about behind the prisoners, divided from them by a raised way upon which is built a low wall.

Above and behind both the prisoners and men burns a fire whose light casts the shadows seen by the prisoners upon the wall opposite.

Socrates states that this story is a metaphor of the human condition.

Man, like the prisoners, witnesses the fire of divine truth at several removes and thus inhabits and experiences a mere semblance of true reality.

Man has become separated from the "real" light of truth, the transcendent realm of the Gods. Platonic philosophy promises that after a series of reincarnations such a state of unity may be reattained.

For Aristotle, the question of Being depended upon the notion of "substance" – that which endures through time and change, and which cannot be taken apart and put together again, nor broken up into more of the same kind (as stones can be broken into stones).

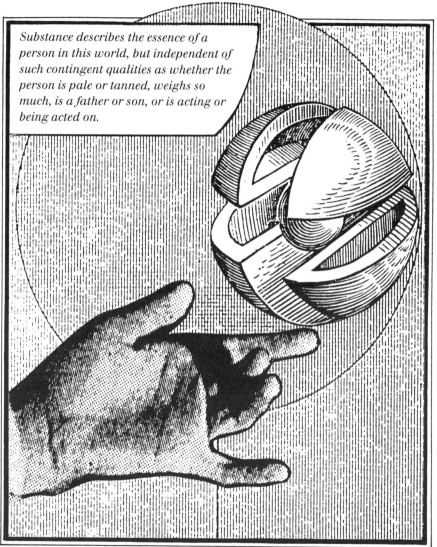

Substance describes the essence of a person in this world, but independent of such contingent qualities as whether the person is pale or tanned, weighs so much, is a father or son, or is acting or being acted on.

Aristotle believed in a God ("the unmoved mover"), creator of the universe's movement. His theory of substance – the idea of humans as receptacles of an indefinable yet necessary **property** – is not necessarily commensurate with a Platonic notion of **transcendental** essence.

Like Platonism, Christian theology is also organized around a hierarchical opposition between the notion of a divine **transcendent** realm and a **corporeal** world. For both beliefs, the transcendent realm is equated with Truth and Essence, whilst the corporeal world is a site of – relative – falsity or Appearance.

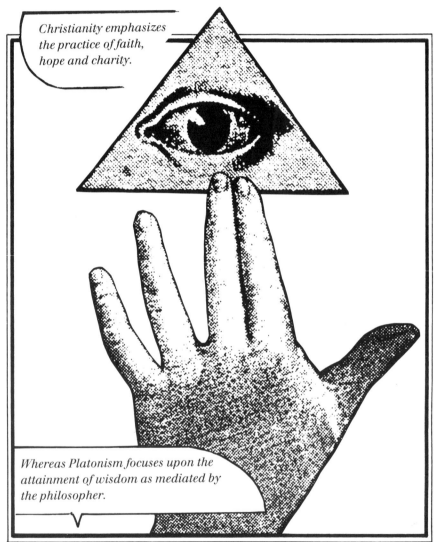

However, despite these differences, both systems rely upon the same fundamental precept whereby Truth as a divine absolute is temporarily removed from Man, yet remains reattainable.

Platonism and Christianity revolve around a central paradox which, on the one hand, maintains a concept of an absolute (the transcendental), and on the other, attempts to sustain the idea that there are realms or sites which are distinct from the absolute. This applies to the phenomenal or corporeal realm, which is supposedly disconnected from the absolute.

It is also applicable to the realm of Hell which in Christianity is designated as a site from which no redemption is possible – and is therefore an **absence** of Being or non-Being.

Platonism also possesses an equivalent concept to the Christian idea of Hell. This is the **simulacral** which refers to the absolute falsity of the Sophist philosopher.

René Descartes (1596–1650) attempted to resolve the paradox of metaphysics by shifting emphasis to the question of consciousness, exemplified in his famous tautological proposition, "I think therefore I am" (***Méditations***, 1641). Descartes ended up repeating metaphysical dialectics. Consciousness, or **reason** as an autonomous being, is substituted for the transcendental object. However, consciousness is paradoxically also conceived of in terms of **becoming**.

*Consciousness is not a property of the mind or senses, but one of actions. I describe acts of **becoming** conscious, not acts of a consciousness.*

Descartes' achievement lay principally in the way he changed the terms of reference of metaphysics, introducing a sense of scepticism and placing greater emphasis upon the question of the human subject and free will. "The will, or freedom of choice which I experience in myself is so great that the idea of any greater faculty is beyond my grasp."

Gottfried Wilhelm von Leibniz (1646–1716) proposed that the universe consists of **Monads**, an infinite set of independent substances in each of which a life force is present, in order to explore the "body and soul" duality. "Bodies act as if there were no souls . . . and souls act as if there were no bodies, and both act as if each influenced the other." (***The Monadology***, 1714)

Monads are the true atoms of nature . . . they are the elements of things. Monads have no windows through which anything could enter or depart.

Monads are subject to change by virtue of "an internal principle" which encompasses memory and perception, yet they are programmed by God to change in synchrony with the world.

Christian Wolff (1679–1754) – whose work was used in Kant's teaching as set reading – attempted to combine Leibnizian Rationalism and Newtonian science. Wolff accepted that much about Nature remained unknown, but that the underlying laws of Nature could be discovered through rationalistic, philosophical principles.

> *Philosophy must possess complete certitude. For since philosophy is a science, its content must be demonstrated by inferring conclusions with legitimate sequence from certain and immutable principles.* (**Preliminary Discourse on Philosophy in General**, 1728)

An example of such a principle is, "in a given case the effect which is attributed to a cause is proportionate to it". Wolff's philosophy is often characterized as dogmatic. Yet, within the history of the problematic of metaphysics, it can be seen to waver uncertainly.

Is reason founded upon valid, transcendental principles, or is it an autonomous and independent system? This was the problematic that I inherited.

Kant's Early Career

Largely for economic reasons, Kant left Königsberg in 1747 to work in the surrounding countryside as a domestic tutor or *Hauslehrer*. Kant was later to say that he was perhaps the worst private tutor the world had ever known!

In 1755, the year following his return to Königsberg, Kant gained his Masters degree and the right to teach as a *Privatdozent*.

This meant that I was permitted to give lectures in the university and to charge students a fee. I only received the public salary of a professor in 1770.

Kant held his first lecture in the autumn of 1755, in a professor's house, "packed with an almost incredible crowd of students".

In keeping with contemporary philosophical interests, Kant was required to teach a broad curriculum of subjects.

Not only logic, metaphysics and ethics, but also politics, physics, natural history, pure and applied mathematics, history, geography, aesthetics, and ancient and modern languages.

He lectured a minimum of sixteen hours a week, with additional seminars and tutorials.

He paints a melancholy picture of his life as a *Privatdozent* in a letter of 1759. "I sit daily at the anvil of my lectern and guide the heavy hammer of my repetitious lectures, always beating out the same rhythm . . . I make do finally with the applause I receive and the benefits I derive from that, dreaming my life away."

One of Kant's early biographers suggests an entirely happier picture. "Kant in his early years spent almost every midday and evening outside his house in social activities, frequently taking part also in a card party and only getting home around midnight. If he was not busy at meals, he

ate in the inn at a table sought out by a number of cultured people." Another contemporary said about the young Kant that, although he had numerous ideas for publication, he was so involved in the "whirl of social diversions" that he was "quite unlikely ever to finish any of them". Kant for a long time also ate almost every day with the officers of the Königsberg garrison. General von Meyer, the chief of staff, employed Kant to instruct the officers in mathematics, physical geography, and fortification.

Early Pre-Critical Work from 1746 to 1770

In this period, Kant tried to find a defence for metaphysics in response to criticisms arising from developments in science. He then found he was unable to justify the rationalist methods used in metaphysics, and even began to question metaphysics itself.

Eventually, I realized I would need to formulate my own concept of metaphysics and related methodology – which I pursued after this period in my three **Critiques** *of* **Pure Reason,** **Practical Reason** *and* **Judgement.**

As a means of confronting the dichotomy between science and metaphysics, Kant in his early work from 1746–59 wrote principally on the subject of natural philosophy (chemistry, cosmology, geology, meteorology, etc.).

Kant's ideas on this subject were often idiosyncratic and highly speculative.

I had the idea that volcanic explosions could change the direction of the earth's axis . . .

. . . that the earth's rotational period was increasing, owing to the friction of the tides against the seabed caused by the moon.

In his writings on cosmology, he tried to reconcile Newton's so-called mechanistic views with the idea of divine presence. Kant supported the idea of an infinite universe and tried to compose "mechanistic" models of its duration and existence.

In *Thoughts on the True Estimation of Living Forces* (1747), Kant devised the model of an infinite three-dimensional universe consisting of worlds rising, decaying, and rising anew for an infinite stretch of aeons. In his *Universal Natural History and Theory of the Heavens* (1755), he changed this image of the universe into a series of concentric waves or rings, of which the "crests" were the regions of fully formed worlds, whereas the "troughs" were the regions of chaos succeeding one another.

I argue that there is a God precisely because nature can proceed even in chaos in no other way than regularly and orderly.

In **New Elucidation of the First Principles of Metaphysical Cognition** (1755), Kant reopened the Aristotelian inquiry into the form and structure of the process by which a concept is defined by a **predicate**. In logic, a predicate is what is affirmed or denied of a subject. For example, in "all men are mortal", **mortal** is the predicate.

Kant was aided in this project by Aristotle's and Christian Wolff's ideas.

Aristotle's "principle of contradiction" is described in *Metaphysics* as the most "certain" and "indisputable" of principles: "the same attribute cannot at the same time belong and not belong to the same subject in the same respect".

Wolff's statement, "something cannot simultaneously be and not be", is a further attempt to suggest that the concept is always already defined by its predicate in a plane of temporal simultaneity.

In the **Inaugural Dissertation, On the Form and Principles of the Sensible and Intelligible World** (1770), Kant changed the definition of metaphysics from "the science of substantial forces" to the science of the "*limits of human reason*". By means of this redefinition, Kant suggested that the fundamental answers to science lie in the **reflexive** analysis of the concept-predicate relationship. ("Reflexive" signifies the subject's action or reflection on itself.) Space and time are conceived of as the fundamental elements of such reflexivity. They provide the conditions for **experience**.

This formal principle of our intuition (space and time) is the condition under which anything can be an object of our senses.

Yet space and time can only be *intuited*. This means that spatial and temporal relations are only experienced by the passive, receptive part of the mind (which Kant calls **intuition**), as opposed to the active part concerned with the **intellect**.

This is why the limits of the mind are often mistakenly taken to be the limits of things in the world.

Nevertheless, the intellect is capable of synthesizing experience. It also grants knowledge of **noumena** – things as they are "in themselves".

Kant's idea of philosophy as an end in itself, with reference to knowledge, formed the basis for the first *Critique,* the **Critique of Pure Reason**. The same idea applied to morality supplied the central component of the second **Critique of Practical Reason**. Kant's ideas on this subject were aided by **Jean-Jacques Rousseau** (1712–78).

Rousseau's writings, such as **The Social Contract** (1762), are centrally concerned with questions of subjective and communal responsibility and duty. Rousseau contrasts Man in a "state of nature" with Man as a "corporate and collective person". For Rousseau, any communal agreement or resolution is the subject of the "General Will" and, as such, reaffirms the need, if not the desire, to regulate relations.

When in the popular assembly a law is proposed, what the people are asked is not precisely whether they accept or reject the proposal, but whether it is in conformity with the general will, which is their will.

Rousseau posits the idea that the "General Will" always awaits discovery; however, "proposals" of law indicate the possibility of its presence.

Rousseau's crucial influence may have been one reason why Kant later dismissed his own early writings in a letter to his publisher J.H. Tieftrunk, 3 October 1797, saying about a prospective edition of his published works, "I would not want you to start the collection with anything before 1770".

Kant acknowledged Rousseau's influence in his annotations to his copy of his treatise, **Observations on the Feeling of the Beautiful and the Sublime** (1764), in which he states that "Rousseau set me right".

I feel a consuming thirst for knowledge . . . There was a time when I thought that this alone could constitute the honour of mankind . . . but one consideration alone gives worth to all the others, namely to establish the rights of man.

In order to accomplish this project, Kant set out to affirm the limits of desire, that is, a duty yet to be named. This is taken up in the second *Critique of Practical Reason*.

Period of Silence, 1770–80

Having staked out his areas of inquiry, Kant began work for ten years, developing a "wholly new science" which culminated in the first *Critique*. This period from 1770–80 is known as the "Silent Decade", since Kant published very little during this time.

Over these years, Kant struggled to realize his ideas – often convinced he was near the end of his task, only to find it was not complete. Kant wrote a letter to his former pupil Marcus Herz, 21 February 1772, stating that . . .

*I am in a position to bring out a **Critique of Pure Reason** . . . and to publish it within three months.*

It was not until nine years later, in 1781, that the first *Critique* was finally published!

During this period, Kant read the "Empiricist" philosophy of **David Hume** (1711–76). Hume's ***A Treatise of Human Nature*** (1739–40) had a decisive impact upon his ideas. He realized that Empiricism and Rationalism (Leibniz, Wolff) could be combined to effect.

I suggested that Empiricism is concerned with habit rather than with the formulation of new experiences – i.e., how and why the subject uses past observations and experiences in order to create relationships or associations.

Habit is nothing but one of the principles of nature, and derives all its force from that.

According to Empiricism, habit arises as a consequence of knowledge which happens after, or succeeds, contact with sensation: it is *a posteriori*.

This does not mean that knowledge is based upon sensation, since the mind resembles a string-instrument, where after each stroke the vibrations still retain some sound.

The echo-like effect of knowledge is a consequence of the general action of principles of reflection within the depths of the mind. Thus, habit relies upon, and testifies to, the action of knowledge, but remains incommensurate with it.

According to Leibniz, Rationalism proposes that knowledge is analytic.

It attempts to anticipate experience by constructing systems of logical deduction from basic axioms.

This rests upon the possibility of pre-given – *a priori* – ideas of reason, e.g. of God and infinity. These ideas cannot be represented, yet nevertheless they remain the preconditions for inquiry into the existence of God or the infinity of numbers. Hence, knowledge is achieved in the difference between the failure of **representation** and the demand or desire to represent.

By considering both Empiricism and Rationalism, Kant created a sophisticated model of knowledge which overcame the simplistic notion of the subject either anticipating or reacting to experience. Hence, he writes in the *Critique of Pure Reason* . . .

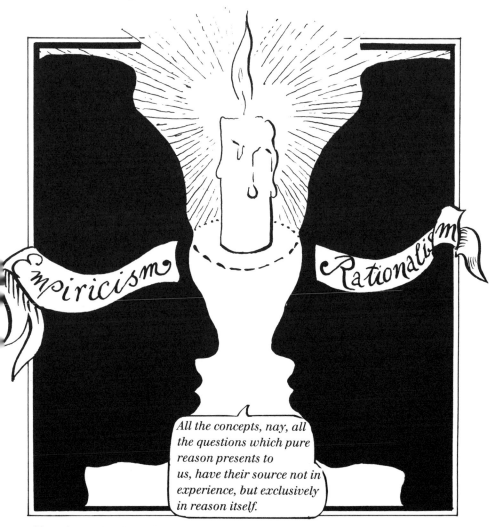

All the concepts, nay, all the questions which pure reason presents to us, have their source not in experience, but exclusively in reason itself.

Kant determined his philosophical project as a **criticism** of reason itself: "a critique, not a doctrine, of pure reason", and the utility of such a critique "ought properly to be only **negative**". By means of "negative criticism", Kant aimed to expunge any fantasy that knowledge can be self-identical or **present** to itself. This can be explained through the concepts of **presence** and **absence**.

The concept of presence is equivalent to the metaphysical concepts of absolute Being and divine Essence, which are equated with Truth. Metaphysics relies emphatically upon a concept of presence. Yet it also depends upon absence: the (relative) absence of Being from the phenomenal or corporeal world, as well as the (absolute) absence of Being from Hell or the simulacral. Both concepts depend upon each other. This paradox can be referred to as a **dialectic**, wherein each term – presence (plus) and absence (minus) – implies the other, such that neither of them can be given an absolute identity. The failure fully to conceptualize or conceive of absence, other than in terms of an implied relation to presence, converts this concept into a notion of "lack" (i.e. lack of presence). As a consequence, neither presence nor absence can be fully thought or substantiated.

This makes any description or representation problematic, as it always depends on the absence of what it appears to make present. The paradox of metaphysical philosophies is that they depend upon the possibility of representing Being and claiming the right to make such representations. Yet, from a logical point of view, the notion of representation cannot be reconciled with the concept of an absolute Being. If the absolute exists, it exists absolutely, outside the dialectic of presence and absence. This would preclude the very possibility of, and need for, representation.

The fundamental theological controversies within Christian thought and practice can be seen to stem from the foregoing paradox.

These controversies and differences stem from the impossibility of reconciling the concept of an absolute Being (or object) with a concept of representation.

Kant's philosophy recognizes the dialectical nature and limits of metaphysics. He proposes that (the concepts of) God or Man cannot be thought (i.e. represented), let alone proven. However, Kant persists with the problem of the inability to prove absolute existence in the *Critique of Pure Reason*. He seeks out . . .

. . . the conditions which make it necessary to regard the non-existence of a thing as absolutely unthinkable.

The consequence of this is Kant's reorganization of the traditional metaphysical duality between the transcendental and corporeal realms into a duality between **noumena** and **phenomena**.

Noumena are the nature of "things in themselves". In effect, they are delimited since they cannot be known. (This contrasts with Kant's pre-Critical work.) Phenomena, or things as they appear to perception, establish the realm of possibility for making judgements concerning the necessity of delimiting noumena.

Such judgements would possess an absolute and objective value. Philosophy's task would be continually to engage with, and frustrate, any claim for knowledge's relation to presence.

Thus, Kant defines philosophy in the *Critique of Pure Reason* as "the science of the relation of all knowledge to the essential ends of human reason", or as "the love which the reasonable being has for the supreme ends of human reason". This means that philosophy's aim ("end") is now entirely bound up with its own impossibility as knowledge in a metaphysical sense. Kant's introduction of negative criticism into the programme of philosophy can thus be seen as an essentially **modern** step.

CRITICAL PHILOSOPHY

Introduction: The Faculties

Kant develops his ideas in the Critical philosophy through a network of **faculties**. Aristotle was the first philosopher to explore the concept of the faculties in any detail.

*In the **Metaphysics**, the faculties are utilized as the means of defining different agencies of the soul in nature (plants, animals), man and God.*

Aristotle did not make a clear distinction between the soul and body, but argued that there were different kinds of soul. The minimal soul is the *nutritive,* which exists in plants and animals alike. Next comes the *sensitive* soul, which exists in all animals. This soul is capable of *perception* (touch, taste, smell, hearing, sight). The sensitive soul is further organized into faculties for *feeling* pleasure and pain (and therefore desire), *imagination* (including memory) and *movement*. Man possesses all these faculties, as well as a faculty of *reason*.

Aristotle attributed two senses to the concept of faculties: these refer to a power or ability to achieve an end (as in an aim), and the power for change (potentiality). The dual definition of faculty as *potentiality* and as a *power of the mind* persists in Descartes and Wolff.

In the three great texts of Critical philosophy, published between 1781 and 1790, Kant develops the creative tension that exists within this dualistic definition. He assigns the soul different attributes, each of which is a power in itself.

These are *knowledge,* ethical and moral *desire* and *feeling* (pleasure and displeasure). Each of these faculties corresponds to one of the three *Critiques:* the *Critique of Pure Reason* (knowledge), the *Critique of Practical Reason* (desire) and the *Critique of Judgement* (feeling).

The Potential of Judgement

Kant's three faculties denote a revised definition of theological and metaphysical ideas of the soul. For Kant, the soul is "the thinking substance as the principle of life in matter".

Throughout the Critical project, Kant investigates the legitimacy of the tripartite division of the soul, seeking that which is specific to each faculty. The result is that division, itself, becomes the means for reconciling the dualism of power and its potentiality. The principle of division is explored through *judgement*. Each *Critique* sets out to affirm the potential of judgement as a living power: the ability to make the following judgements . . . "This is knowledge" (first *Critique*), and "One ought to act in a particular way" (second *Critique*).

*The third **Critique** examines the power of judgement itself, communicated through feelings of pleasure and displeasure.*

The judgement, "This is beautiful" is connected to the former emotion.

*There is no judgement **per se** which corresponds to the latter emotion, displeasure.*

Three Cognitive Faculties

These judgements are all phrased in an anonymous way: they do not belong to an individual or collective *subject*. Furthermore, these judgements are not made about an *object* or thing. Rather, they represent that which is irreducible to an object, through which the subject is realized.

> *Each of the faculties of the soul is developed through a further set of cognitive faculties.*

There are three active faculties: *imagination*, *understanding* and *reason*, and one receptive faculty: *sensible intuition* (Kant often conflates this faculty with imagination).

This second set of faculties replaces the idea of an *individual* psyche with an abstracted *schema* designed to overcome both related metaphysical dichotomies of presence and absence, as well as subject and object. (See presence and absence discussed on page 51.)

Imagination and Reflexivity

Kant does not assume a *transcendental* object (an unknown and unknowable, e.g. God) or an *empirical* object (nature) as the ground or purpose of philosophy. Rather, the faculties of understanding, imagination and reason are envisaged primarily as processes, each of which depends upon the others.

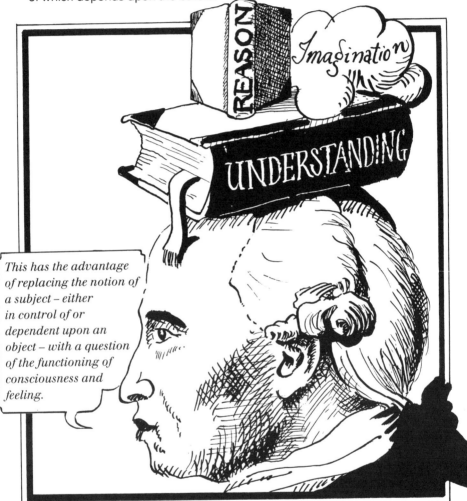

This has the advantage of replacing the notion of a subject – either in control of or dependent upon an object – with a question of the functioning of consciousness and feeling.

The faculty of imagination is a device for intuiting data (which Kant calls "phenomena" or "manifold") and, by means of this, presenting the possibility of **reflexivity** to the faculty of understanding. Yet, in presenting this possibility, imagination cannot possess an identity of its own. "Imagination is the faculty of representing in intuition an object that is *not itself present*."

Understanding, Representation and Reason

The faculty of understanding is involved in processes of classification and ordering data presented to it by the faculty of imagination. This is not necessarily a process of comprehension, but rather of *representation*.

Therefore, the faculty of understanding, like the faculty of imagination, is not capable of thinking *to* or *for itself*.

Reason, as "the faculty of principles", retains the question of transcendental or universal value in terms of three **Ideas** (a term adapted from Plato's concept of transcendent pure Ideas). They are the *soul*, the *cosmos* and *God*.

*These **a priori** Ideas are utilized by the faculty of understanding as the way of attempting to organize and make sense of the information provided by the faculty of imagination.*

The faculty of reason's Ideas are "unconditioned", meaning that they are unrepresentable *in* and *to themselves*, yet also operative for realizing the respective processes of the faculties of imagination and understanding. This means that the Ideas of reason exist as permanent ideals by virtue of the functioning of the other two faculties.

THE CRITIQUE OF PURE REASON (1781)

Introduction: The Problem of Representation

During the period of pre-Critical work, Kant increasingly sensed the dialectical nature of metaphysics and applied himself to a reconsideration of its limits. In a letter to Marcus Herz, on 21 February 1772, Kant writes about his plans for the *Critique of Pure Reason*.

The key to the whole secret of hitherto still obscure metaphysics is to be found in the question, "What is the ground of the relation of that in us which we call 'representation' to the object?"

Yet, Kant rejects "the object" in metaphysical terms.

For him, there is no longer a concept of presence, so absence loses its connotation of negation (absence of presence), as metaphysics had formerly proposed.

*Representation now has nothing to **represent**. It is subsumed by absence. In fact, it **is** absence, since there is nothing else.*

Yet, because absence is non-categorizable, and beyond any point of comparison or contrast (with presence), it must also be irreducible.

The Uncertainties of Representation

Representation is therefore unstable, oscillating between two different functions . . .
1) a representation of or about a concept: either the transcendental and/or the empirical "object". . .
2) and/or as the transcendental conditions or "ground" of representation.

In other words, representation may exist as both "the object" and a representation of "the object".

Philosophy can describe and represent the nature and conditions of representation, including that of itself. This is why philosophy remains a transcendental project with the power to determine truth *a priori*, i.e. in advance.

The Central Question

Yet philosophy must also be affected by the discords of representation in unpredictable ways. This is why philosophy is *synthetic*. Synthetic means . . .

1) **Additive.** Philosophy adds to, or extends, previous knowledge.

2) **Productive.** Philosophy develops knowledge of "the outside". It produces, and is produced by, heterogeneous relations with alterity (otherness).

The central question of the first **Critique** *is: "How are* **a priori** *synthetic judgements possible?"*

However, in so far as philosophy is in a position to represent judgements concerning knowledge, it must guard against its own fantasies and illusions of itself, and maintain a reflexive relationship with itself. Hence the concept of "critique", announced in the title of the book. In as much as it can achieve this project, then it has the right to call itself a transcendental philosophy of "pure reason".

The Transcendental Aesthetic

The first main section of the *Critique of Pure Reason* is entitled "The Transcendental Aesthetic".

Kant is concerned with sensibility or sensible intuition, for which the faculty of imagination is responsible. Sensibility is a passive power for receiving data. Kant is solely concerned with the *form* this data takes rather than with its *matter*. Unlike the tradition of metaphysics, he is not concerned with what the data might be and what it represents.

The Role of Form

Form enables intuition's representations to be cognized by the faculty of understanding. Hence, Kant's task is twofold.
1) To isolate that which is specific to intuition.
2) And paradoxically, to discover a relationship between understanding and that which is specific to intuition.

Space and Time

Understanding cognizes form through *space* and *time*.

This depended on form being cognizable as an object, and it is this "presence" which Kant questions. For him, form is *formed through*, and therefore *is*, space and time.

The Absences of Space and Time

Since Kant does not assume a metaphysical concept of presence, space is the *void* and time is *infinite time* – i.e. absences of space and time.

However, absence is irreducible and other than itself. Hence, space does not occupy space, but nor can it disappear; and time does not suffer alteration in time, yet it cannot cease. Neither is present to itself.

We can never represent to ourselves the absence of space, though we can quite well think it as empty of objects. Appearances may one and all vanish, but time (as the universal condition of their possibility) cannot be removed.

Traditionally, space and time are thought of as the conditions of the existence of things, operating as all-encompassing eternal elements. Kant changes this idea and proposes that space and time cannot exist, because the void and infinity are incapable of being thought. It is only by virtue of the very fact that they cannot be thought, that they exist as the *a priori* "conditions of the existence of things".

Two Operations of Imagination: Apprehension and Reproduction

The faculty of imagination, in tandem with sensible intuition, engages in a "synthesis" of the "manifold" (or data).

"I understand by synthesis the act of arranging different representations together."

Form, as space and time, is reproduced in order to attain this synthesis. This is achieved through two operations of imagination: **apprehension** and **reproduction**.

These two operations are the very mechanisms of thought, producing and reproducing data for representation, although, in themselves, they always exceed imagination: the imagination cannot imagine or "comprehend" itself. This is why it is in a position to represent its findings to the understanding and "comprehend what is manifold under one form of knowledge".

Understanding and Intuition

In the section entitled "The Transcendental Analytic", Kant analyses how the faculty of understanding makes the data presented by the faculty of imagination into so-called objects of thought. "Without sensibility no object would be given to us, without understanding no object would be thought."

Imagination functions as a passive foil, by which understanding may realize itself – as dependent upon imagination.

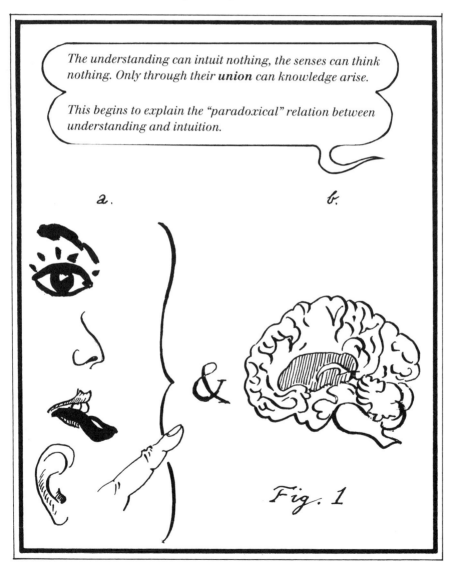

Fig. 1

The Categories

Whereas imagination is "receptive", understanding is a "power" to form concepts (also called **categories**). "The understanding knows all that it knows by concepts only." These represent and order the data given by imagination.

I took over the notion of category outlined in Aristotle's book, the **Categories**.

I listed ten categories. These are meant to define every possible form of predication.

4. _relation_ (e.g. double)

3. _quality_ (e.g. white)

1. _substance_ (e.g. man)

6. _time_ (e.g. yesterday)

9. _action_ (e.g. cuts)

10. _passivity_ (e.g. is cut)

2. _quantity_ (e.g. two cubits long)

8. _possession_ (e.g. wears shoes)

7. _position_ (e.g. sitting)

5. _place_ (e.g. in the Lyceum)

Kant's Four Categories

Kant reorganized his concepts (or categories) alongside a corresponding table of judgements. They consist of four types: **quantity**, **quality**, **relation** and **modality**. In this scheme he approaches the question of the relationship between concept and predicate (see page 31).

The predicate – i.e. the condition upon which a concept depends – includes all, some or one of its subjects (**quantity**).
The predicate applies to some subjects and not others (**quality**).
The predicate could apply to all or some subjects and not others (**relation**).
Importantly, this leaves open the question of whether or not the predicate is contained within the concept (Kant refers to this situation in terms of **modality**).

How Does Understanding Occur?

Kant's tables demonstrate the different ways in which a concept can be related to a predicate. Yet they also show that the function of the predicate, as a process of *defining* knowledge, is fundamentally different from the question of the predicate as a *source* of knowledge, as was believed by traditional metaphysics.

Understanding occurs in the difference between process and knowledge.

Understanding may seem to be in a hopeless situation, forever condemned to order information and speculate over the origins and causation of its knowledges (as given in the question, "Upon what is knowledge predicated?").

But Kant does not take a pessimistic or tragic view. Principally, because understanding is unable to ascribe the source of knowledge to imagination, even though it realizes a sense of dependency through using the categories.

Kant's "Copernican Revolution"

Copernicus (1473–1543) displaced a human-centred universe by suggesting that the earth revolves around the sun. Kant introduced a schism between Man and (his) consciousness by suggesting that consciousness is no longer defined by, or answerable to, a transcendental or empirical object (a situation in which "knowledge must conform to objects").

This answers Kant's question, "*Quid facti*?" (What is the fact of knowledge?).

Kant proposes that the synthesis between a predicate and concept *is brought into being* by understanding. This gives understanding a legislative right over the other two faculties, and answers Kant's question, "*Quid juris*?" (What right does knowledge possess?).

How Images (Data) Become Possible

"Pure reason leaves everything to the understanding – the understanding alone applying immediately to the objects of intuition, or rather to their synthesis in the imagination."

Kant stamps understanding's legislative power with a "monogram", termed a "schematism", which resides in imagination.

The schematism affirms that images (i.e. the data) presented by imagination are irreducible, and hence discoverable and representable as language (the letters of the monogram) by the understanding. Nevertheless, the schematism remains a process – "an art concealed in the depths of the human soul, whose real modes of activity nature is hardly likely ever to allow us to discover, and to have open to our gaze".

Understanding and Apperception

Self-consciousness – the awareness that "*I think*" – arises in understanding's recognition or **apperception** that it is entirely separate from imagination, yet already implicated within, and generative of, its processes.

*I call it **pure apperception** . . . because it is that self-consciousness which, while generating the representation "I think" . . . cannot itself be accompanied by any further representation.*

Understanding obtains the right to apply its concepts to all objects of possible experience through reason's "Ideas" which go beyond the possibility of experience.

Kant states that reason says, "Everything happens *as if* . . . ". Reason exists as an absolute condition of all conditions, yet this does not restrict understanding from applying variable concepts to objects of possible experience. Everything happens to, and for, understanding as if reason is *absent*.

The absence of reason guarantees that everything happens. However, without a metaphysical object to represent, this means **nothing happens!** Nothing becomes active – without subject or object.

As Kant reaches the point of affirming that "nothing happens", he also recognizes that nothing *ever* happens for the subject to witness or represent. The subject is dispossessed from the event of nothing happening, as even that is absent by the very act of thinking and affirming it. This is what seems inconceivable: that the thought of "nothing" is different from nothing "itself" – or that "process" is different from "object", and "concept" is different from "Idea".

The Help of Reason

Understanding cannot deal on its own with this abstract *a priori* idea of nothing. It requires the help of the faculty of reason, although this does not affect its supremacy over reason and imagination.

The function of the faculty of reason is both to submit, as well as to give itself, to the faculty of understanding.

Since reason does not function within determinable boundaries, its dual operations of submission and giving are not ascribable to a munificent, divine or transcendental source.

By virtue of reason's operations, understanding obtains the right to legislate over the faculties of imagination and reason. Hence, legislation (by understanding) and the affirmation of judgement (also by understanding) are both forms of realizing reason's gift of itself.

The Illusions of Understanding

Kant states that the territory of pure understanding is the "land of truth". However, it is also "the native home of illusion, where many a fog bank and many a swiftly melting iceberg give the deceptive appearance of farther shores, deluding the adventurous seafarer ever anew with empty hopes".

Illusions continually obstruct understanding's reflexive capacity, leading it to confuse the power to *realize* consciousness with the power to *control* consciousness.

False ideas arise as a consequence of an improper consideration of reason's Ideas.

The Paralogisms of Pure Reason

In another section of the *Critique*, entitled "Transcendental Dialectic", Kant shows how false ideas can occur with regard to reason's ideas of the *soul*, the *cosmos* and *God*. Let's begin with a false idea of the soul which can arise through "the paralogisms of pure reason", that is, through reasoning by *premise* and *conclusion*.

Kant lists four fallacies which can be derived from understanding's judgement, "I think". Each depends on "a transcendental ground" which nevertheless leads to "a formally invalid conclusion".

In each case, the premise is speculative. This affirms the notion of the subject, but only in so far as the subject is constituted in the difference between a) being separated from its own consciousness and b) being separated from consciousness in general.

1. *Premise*: "Necessarily, the subject of thought is a subject."
2) *Conclusion*: "The subject of thought is necessarily a subject."

1. *Premise*: "The ego cannot be divided into parts."
2. *Conclusion*: "The ego is a simple substance."

1. *Premise*: "Whenever I am conscious, it is the same I who am conscious."
2. *Conclusion*: "Whenever I am conscious, I am conscious of the same I."

1. *Premise*: "I can think of myself apart from everything, including my body."
2. *Conclusion*: "Apart from every other thing including my body, I can think of myself."

The conclusion tries to stabilize the premise, such that the subject is falsely conceived of as **autonomous.**

The Antinomy of Pure Reason

Next, a false idea of the cosmos can arise through "the antinomy of pure reason", that is, through reasoning by **thesis** and **antithesis**. Kant lists four of these supposedly opposed arguments or antinomies.

Thesis: "The world has a beginning in time, and is also limited as regards space."

Thesis: "Nothing anywhere exists save the simple or what is composed of the simple".

Thesis: "Causality is in accordance with laws of nature and freedom."

Thesis: "There belongs to the world, either as its part or as its cause, a being that is absolutely necessary."

The antinomies bring out the mismatch between the scope of empirical enquiry and the pretensions of the rational ideal. The theses represent the world as *limited*, yet dependent upon ideas of infinity and the absolute; the antitheses conflate the *infinity* of the world with the absolute.

*In presenting the antinomy, I hoped to shake reason from the slumber of **fictitious** conviction.*

Antithesis: "The world has no beginning, and no limits in space; it is infinite as regards both time and space."

Antithesis: "There nowhere exists in the world anything simple."

Antithesis: "There is no freedom; everything in the world takes place solely in accordance with the laws of nature."

Antithesis: "An absolutely necessary being nowhere exists in the world, nor does it exist outside the world as its cause."

The Ideal of Pure Reason

A false idea of God can arise via the "Ideal of Pure Reason", that is, through reasoning by **ontology** (the nature of being), **cosmology** and **psycho-theology**, which propose to establish the existence of God.

1) Arguments from **ontology** take their cue from the *a priori* concept of a Supreme Being.
2) Arguments from **cosmology** derive from the nature of an empirical world in general.
3) Arguments from **psycho-theology** start from particular natural phenomena.

*I dispute all three theories. As with the paralogisms and the antinomies, the ideals of pure reason claim to know something determinate. They confuse understanding's power to **make** judgements of thought with the power to **know** the transcendental object.*

Kant remains sceptical about providing knowledge either of the existence or non-existence of God.

From what source will the freethinker derive his professed knowledge that there is no supreme being? This proposition is outside the field of all possible experience, and therefore beyond the limits of human insight.

In making claims to know, or not know, an object corresponding to the Ideas, reason remains in a "state of nature" which is akin to a state of war. Peace reigns in a perfect civil state, accompanied by the exercise of natural law, when reason is subject to critique. "The greatest and perhaps sole use of all philosophy of pure reason has only the modest merit of guarding against error."

Through critique, the question of the transcendental survives, and reason's giving of itself to understanding remains of value.

Kant's Middle Years

Kant finally rose from *Privatdozent* to obtain a chair as Professor of Logic and Metaphysics in 1770. A professorship meant that he now received a public salary and no longer depended on fees paid by students.

It also meant I could give up my position as sub-librarian at the royal castle of King Frederick William II which I'd gained in 1765.

Kant became a leading figure for advocating a reconsideration of the status of philosophy at the University of Königsberg. He also believed in the public use of Reason – that philosophy should be taught to the youth and the people.

To obtain his chair in philosophy, Kant was required to write a thesis: *On the Form and Principles of the Sensible and Intelligible World*.

This thesis was a pivotal work, summing up the achievements of the 1750s and 1760s and also preparing the ground for the *Critiques* of *Pure Reason* and *Practical Reason*. As prescribed by official university rules, Kant's thesis, and previous ones he had submitted, were written in Latin.

Dining with Professor Kant

In his middle age and later years, Kant entertained friends for lunch every day. These luncheons frequently ran on through the afternoon until four or five o'clock. His guests were made up of high-ranking people: generals, aristocrats, bank directors and merchants.

At these luncheons, I rarely talked about my own work, preferring to discuss other topics, especially politics and the sciences.

One of Kant's acquaintances, R.B. Jachman, gives an account of his culinary preferences. "His menus were simple: three courses, followed by cheese. In the summer he ate with the windows open onto the garden. He had a large appetite, and he especially liked meat broths as well as vermicelli and barley soup. Roast meats were always served at table, but never fowl. Usually, Kant began his meals with fish, and accompanied all courses with mustard. He adored cheese, especially English cheeses. Cake was served if the guests were numerous . . . He drank red wine,

usually Medoc, of which a bottle was set before each guest. He also drank white wine, as a way of relieving the astringent after-effects of the red wine. After dinner he drank a glass of dessert wine, which was warmed and scented with orange peel."

Despite these regular friendly luncheons, Kant guarded his privacy jealously. A letter written to his former pupil Marcus Herz in April 1778 reveals his need to restrict social relations. "Monetary gain and the excitement of a grand stage are, as you know, not much of an incentive for me. A peaceful situation nicely fitted to my needs, occupied in turn with work, speculation and my circle of friends, where my mind, which is easily touched but otherwise free of cares, and my body, which is cranky but never ill, are kept busy in a leisurely way without strain, is all that I

have wished for and had. Any change makes me apprehensive, even if it gives the greatest promise of improving my condition, and I am persuaded by this natural instinct of mine that I must take heed if I wish the threads which the Fates spin so thin and weak in my case to be spun to any length. My great thanks, then, to my well-wishers and friends, who think so kindly of me as to undertake my welfare, but at the same time a most humble request to protect me in my present situation from any disturbance."

Kant did not form any close relationship with either sex.

He provided allowances to his brother and sisters, but took care to keep well away from them. He did not see them for twenty-five years, until one of his sisters attended him at his bedside during his last illness.

Kant's life during these years was ordered with the utmost regularity.
Every day, at 4.55 a.m. precisely (i.e. the time just before he was born!),
his valet Lampe, who had served in the Prussian army, marched into his
bedroom and woke him with an ominous cry.

At 5 a.m. he took breakfast, and then spent the morning writing or
lecturing. At 12.15 p.m. he would lunch. During most of his life, the
solitary constitutional which followed luncheon was so exactly timed
that it is said the inhabitants of Königsberg could set their clocks by it.
After the end of his walk, Kant would read till 10 p.m.

The *Critique of Practical Reason* (1788)

Written five years after the end of the American War of Independence and a year before the French Revolution, Kant's *Critique of Practical Reason* deals with the question of freedom and of universal moral law. These issues had deep political resonance in Europe and America at the time.

The German writer **Heinrich Heine** (1797–1856) proposed that the *Critique of Practical Reason* was written by Kant to appease his servant Lampe!

Having demolished religious belief in the first **Critique**, *Kant restored a notion of faith in the second.*

NITY THERE IS STRENGTH

INDEPENDENCE

The second *Critique* has often been read as a text with religious dimensions, particularly in its assertion of moral law. But, contrary to Heine's assessment, it will be found that Kant's conception of moral law remains in keeping with the critical scepticism of his preceding book.

Predestination or Free Will?

The historical and philosophical context for Kant's *Critique of Practical Reason* lies in the debates surrounding the idea of predestination which had been brought to a head by the disputes between **Martin Luther** (1483–1546), **John Calvin** (1509–64) and the Catholic Church in the 16th century. The underlying cause for these disputes lay in the inability of all parties to reconcile a notion of **free will** with the idea of **predestination** (in which the subject had no control over his or her fate). Calvin believed in predestination. Luther and Catholicism argued over the individual's right to make supplications to God as a way of influencing what is to become of the soul.

These disputes continued into the 18th century. Through his Pietist upbringing, Kant was taught to believe in miracles and divine intervention. Such beliefs tended to displace the question of predestination.

Upon encountering rationalist philosophy, I was led to reconsider the vexed question of free will as it pertained to notions of consciousness and spirit.

Rationalism suggested that free will arose in the difference between the production of knowledge (philosophy) and Nature (as that which produces itself). But Rationalism was still forced to sanction this "difference" (i.e. free will) through appeal to a higher Being or Good or Value.

Free Will and Desire

In the second *Critique,* Kant states that "the practical interest" refers to "everything that is possible through freedom". Specifically, it is concerned with free will.

Free will is will which can be determined independently of sensuous impulses. It is considered the only object that is morally good without qualification.

The overriding question of the *Critique of Practical Reason* asks whether there is a higher faculty of desire. "Desire" here means that which is "morally good and useful" in the exercise of free will. This is linked to two further questions: "What ought I to do?" and "What may I hope?"

Moral Examples

Kant is sceptical of providing models for moral behaviour. He finds that so-called exemplary forms of behaviour are invariably fraught with contradictions. Kant cites the case of a man who saves others in a shipwreck, but loses his own life in the process.

In honouring others' lives, he failed to honour his own.

A similar problem arises in regard to a patriotic sacrifice. "More decisive is the magnanimous sacrifice of one's life for the preservation of one's country, and yet there still remain some scruples as to whether it is so perfect a duty to devote oneself spontaneously and unbidden to this purpose." Kant concludes that "the action itself does not have the full force of a model and impulse to imitation".

For Kant, moral contradictions lead to moral dilemmas. He tells the story of a man who is asked by a despotic king to betray an honourable man or face death himself.

Nevertheless, Kant argues that there are recognizable examples of "an inexorable duty" being performed. He cites a passage from the **Satire** VIII, lines 79–84, by the Roman author **Juvenal** (A.D. c. 60–130), "which makes the reader vividly feel the power of the drive which lies in the pure law of duty as duty".

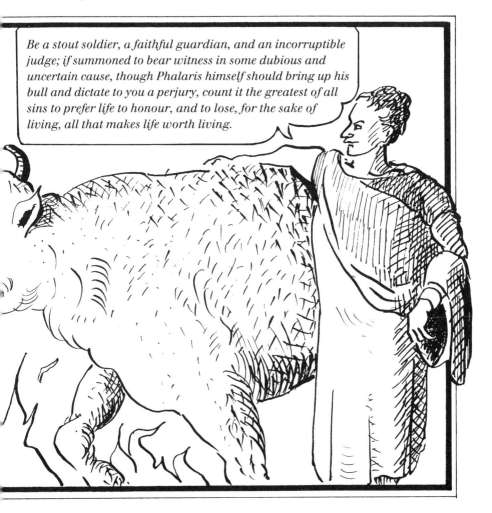

Be a stout soldier, a faithful guardian, and an incorruptible judge; if summoned to bear witness in some dubious and uncertain cause, though Phalaris himself should bring up his bull and dictate to you a perjury, count it the greatest of all sins to prefer life to honour, and to lose, for the sake of living, all that makes life worth living.

Phalaris, tyrant of Agrigentum, had a brass ox constructed in which his victims were burned to death.

For Kant, Juvenal's prescriptions help to strengthen the soul and elevate the mind. But they cannot be taken as a model for moral behaviour.

Just as there are no models for moral behaviour, so it is impossible to provide maxims or axioms containing truisms for moral conduct. Kant wryly observes that such truisms invariably assume that moral behaviour will lead to happiness. Sometimes this is taken so far that "men have thought of proclaiming as a universal practical law the desire for happiness".

If happiness were made the primary object of Man's desires, the consequence would be the extreme opposite of harmony, the most arrant conflict, and the complete annihilation of the maxim itself and its purpose.

Why is that?

Because the wills of all do not have one and the same object, but each person has his own welfare at heart.

By way of illustrating this conflict, Kant cites the pledge made between a married couple going to ruin. "Oh marvellous harmony – what he wants is what she wants!"

The Antinomy of Practical Reason

The problem of establishing happiness as a moral objective is that it cannot be united with moral virtue (i.e. the means by which moral objectives are pursued). This contradiction forms the basis for the "antinomy of practical Reason".

The **thesis** states that "the desire for happiness must be the motive to maxims of virtue".

Whilst the **antithesis** proposes that "the maxim of virtue must be the efficient cause of happiness".

thesis

antithesis

*Both options are untenable. In the first case, because no desire, not even the desire for happiness, can be considered as an **a priori** basis for virtue.*

In the second case, because virtue and happiness cannot be seen to effect each other.

Unconditional Freedom

According to Kant, a moral state depends on freedom, and must arise "spontaneously", outside of a relationship between cause and effect. This means that virtue and happiness cannot be predicated upon each other. The desire to make either one into a predicate for the other would involve a wilful violence upon freedom, by defining it as the third term or condition for the others.

In this way, Kant affirms that freedom *is* free, outside of humanist desires.

The central concern of the second *Critique* is to assert as law that freedom is the unconditional term for the (non-)relation between happiness and virtue. In turn, this has a bearing upon the question of causality and production of the (non-)relation between happiness and virtue.

Kant re-employs the three faculties of **Imagination**, **Understanding** and **Reason** to outline the fundamentally unstable nature of the relationship between **happiness**, **virtue** and **freedom**, in which none of the terms involved can be made into the condition for the others.

This failure of conditionality is the moral law, which, in turn, is always already failing to stabilize into a set of prescriptions for correct behaviour.

Kant's interest in this process of "failure" concerns the *effort* by which the moral law continually succeeds in failing to obtain itself for representation (Understanding). The law, being the law, always *tries* to be the law.

Effort and Sacrifice

This question of the moral law's effort to obtain representation leads Kant to reconceptualize the issue of **sacrifice** (or self-sacrifice) and specifically to re-evaluate Christian notions of sacrifice.

Kant achieves this re-evaluation through examining the functions of the **faculties**, although this time they take on a different relationship to that proposed in the first *Critique*.

Rethinking the Faculties

In the second *Critique*, the faculty of Reason becomes the legislative faculty and imposes a moral law upon the other two faculties of Understanding and Imagination.

*Reason's law is sanctioned by a higher morality, yet it is **also** this higher morality itself.*

Reason=
Legislative
Faculty

Understanding

Imagination

It is both **essence** and **representation**. In so far as it is essence, Reason's law stands apart from the other two faculties, but in as much as it is a representation (of the law) it can be brought into consciousness and organized as a thought by the faculty of Understanding. However, ultimately, this thought fails to cohere with the concepts of the Understanding.

Absolute Absence of Moral Reason

Kant does not ask: how is Reason's law established? Rather, he is able to displace any questioning of its source or origins.

*This is because the law is simultaneously both the source of all laws (as essence, Reason's law is **absolutely absent**) and a representation (Understanding **must** represent the absence of all laws as a law).*

Reason functions as the absolute absence of any moral reason or higher purpose. Since this absence is absolute, Understanding forms a consciousness of the absence of absolute moral reason and higher purpose as a law.

The Limits of Consciousness

As in the first *Critique*, Kant is again forced to circumscribe Understanding's so-called "consciousness". Basically, this "consciousness" must not be seen to form itself into an absolute representation, for if it were to do this it would fall back into a metaphysical contradiction.

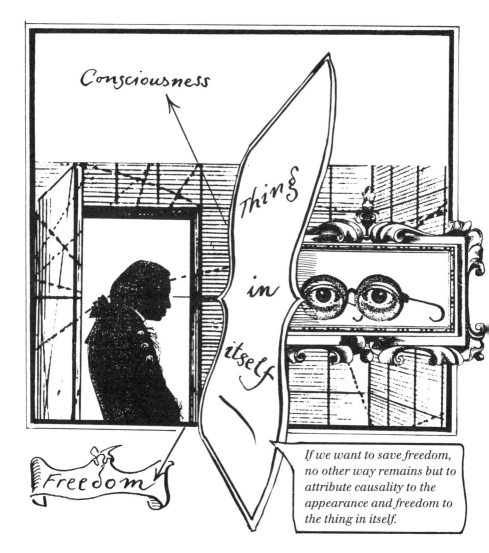

Consciousness

Thing in itself

Freedom

If we want to save freedom, no other way remains but to attribute causality to the appearance and freedom to the thing in itself.

Freedom functions in terms of an Idea of Reason as **noumenon** (thing in itself), whilst Understanding's continuous yet futile search for an objective principle governing freedom is situated in the realm of appearances and illusion.

Pure Freedom and Desire for Knowledge

Kant seems to repeat a traditional metaphysical dichotomy in which freedom is a transcendental principle and the desire for knowledge is lacking in true substance. But this turns out not to be the case. Kant scrutinizes Understanding's helpless and misguided situation. He concludes that this situation demonstrates that a fundamental difference exists between *pure freedom* (Reason) and the *desire for knowledge about freedom* (Understanding).

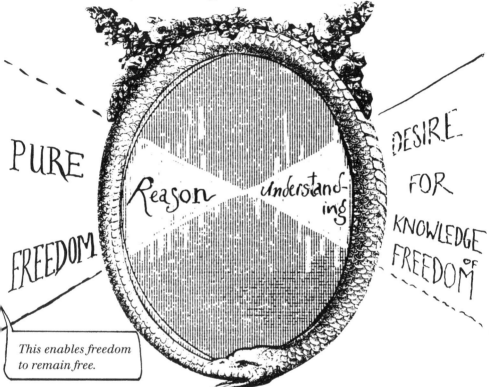

This enables freedom to remain free.

It also keeps the question of causality open, thus assuring that speculation, as prompted in the interaction between Understanding and Imagination, is free.

Failure of Representation

Kant can now rethink the question of absolute freedom. He states that practical reason and freedom are not one and the same. "Practical reason" here means that which represents Understanding's continuous process of misunderstanding: the "consciousness" of the absolute absence of moral purpose in the faculty of Reason.

> In effect, this is the concept of the moral law as the failure of representation.

The concept of moral law is not equivalent to freedom, since freedom cannot be contained within moral law. Rather, freedom is an Idea of speculative Reason.

The Sacrifice of Freedom

The Ideas of speculative Reason were introduced in the *Critique of Pure Reason* and were characterized in terms of three concepts – the Subject as substance, the World as series, and God as system – which were always already sacrificed to the Understanding. Now the concept of freedom is added to these three concepts.

The moral law of the failure of representation does not give rise to a concept of freedom. Rather, freedom is perpetually sacrificed in order to give rise to the moral law of representation as failure.

Although freedom is conceived of as an absolute, it never actually exists as such in the **metaphysical** sense, since its existence is always already conditioned by sacrifice.

The Noumenon or "Thing in Itself"

In the *Critique of Pure Reason*, Understanding possessed a "consciousness" of its inability to form a consciousness of the "thing in itself" (noumenon). The "thing in itself" resided in a site beyond Understanding's consciousness. The very absence of the "thing in itself" allowed Understanding to form a consciousness or representation of something outside itself: *the faculty of Reason*.

Hence, Reason became the means for mediating between Understanding and the "thing in itself".

In other words, Understanding's consciousness of the absence of the "thing in itself" was, in fact, a consciousness of the *absence of Reason*.

Mourning and Sacrifice

It could be said that the purpose of the *Critique of Pure Reason* is to mourn for that which might have presented the "thing in itself" to Understanding, i.e. Reason.

In the *Critique of Practical Reason*, the situation is radically changed. Understanding no longer possesses a "consciousness" of Reason as such: the representations of the Understanding are always already shattered and broken apart. This is because a reciprocity develops between Understanding and Reason which does not allow for a sense of grieving or mourning. The faculty of Reason as an "object" of grief for Understanding has entirely disappeared.

*All that remains is the **sacrifice of Reason**.*

Suffering the Absence of Reason

This sacrifice of Reason is not received by Understanding in terms of a debt or even a sense of gratitude, as Christianity views Christ's sacrifice. Instead, it is internalized by the Understanding and "represented" more in terms of pain and suffering than grief.

Such feelings of pain are also constituted by the action of the moral law upon Imagination. The "humbling" of Imagination occurs as a consequence of its separation from the other two faculties, in so far as it is now unable to supply Understanding with any form of consciousness. (Otherwise, the role of Imagination is not stressed in the *Critique of Practical Reason*.)

Freedom of the Rational Being

The relationship between Reason and Understanding defines the concept of freedom, although freedom itself still remains apart from this relationship, since it is always already sacrificed. In this respect, Kant attributes freedom to the "thing in itself". Therefore, the noumenon must be thought of as free. For Kant, the possibility of such a thought implies that the subject is free: an intelligent or rational being.

Practical reason is therefore not freedom itself but an *effect* of freedom. Kant calls this particular relationship between practical reason and freedom, the **moral law**.

The Suprasensible System

The moral law mediates between Imagination and Understanding, on the one hand, and Reason on the other.

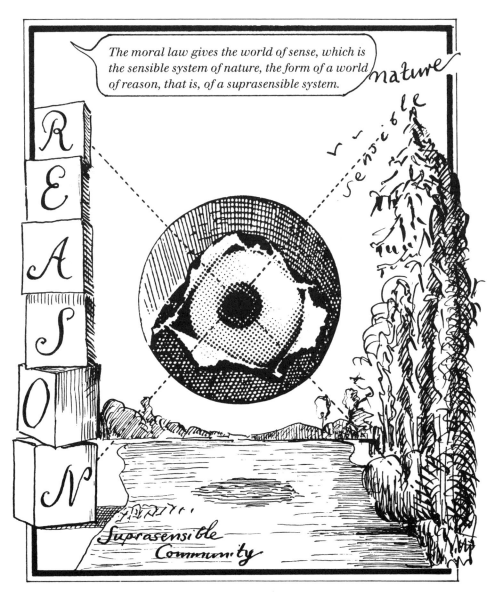

> *The moral law gives the world of sense, which is the sensible system of nature, the form of a world of reason, that is, of a suprasensible system.*

nature

sensible

REASON

Suprasensible Community

The subject must be thought of as a member of an intelligible or *suprasensible community* ("the kingdom of ends") endowed with free causality.

Subject to the Law

Out of the sacrificial relationship between Understanding and Reason, Kant develops firstly, the possibility of a thought (freedom as the "thing in itself") and secondly, a subject who thinks this thought and is therefore a member of a suprasensible community.

In order for these elements to exist, they must be governed by a moral law, that is the law of practical reason.

Thought

FREEDOM

Subject { Supra-sensible Community

But this law does not simply dominate the subject. As a member of "the kingdom of ends", the subject is not only subordinate to the law, but also author of it – both subject and legislator.

Free to Think Freedom

The dignity of man consists precisely in his capacity to make universal law, although only on condition of being himself also subject to the law he makes.

Groundwork of the Metaphysics of Morals, 1785

In other words, the subject is dominated by the thought of freedom, or at least bound to it. But he is also free to think this thought of freedom – he must be absolutely free to think of absolute freedom. In a sense, the subject is the originator of the idea of freedom, because the idea is free and belongs to no one. This is what Kant means when he says the subject is endowed with free causality.

The Categorical Imperative

The "fundamental law of pure practical reason" is known as the **Categorical Imperative**. According to Kant, the command of the categorical imperative is this . . .

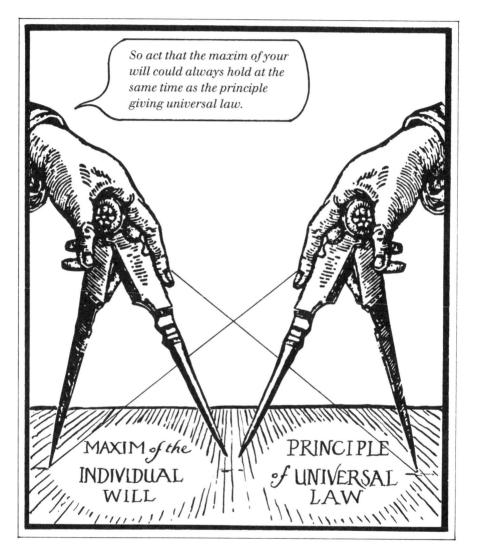

"The principle giving universal law" refers to the form of the difference between the **sensible** and **suprasensible systems** (Imagination/Understanding and Reason). Kant advocates that moral actions are those which affirm this principle, not in the name of freedom (which can never be known), but as an **effect** of freedom.

Avoid Illusion

For Kant, the subject is not to be aligned with either of the faculties of Reason or Understanding. In other words, the subject is not bound either to the process of freedom's sacrifice (Reason) or to the shattering thought of this process (Understanding). Rather, the subject is situated in the difference between process and thought, as well as power and act.

Seek Self-Contentment

Kant warns that correct moral actions are singular and do not produce correct ideas (maxims). The subject should not seek after happiness through action, nor pursue a sensation of bliss by creating or following moral instructions.

> *Rather, the subject must seek self-contentment, which is a negative satisfaction ... in which one is conscious of needing nothing.*

"Needing nothing" is not necessarily meant here in a pious sense, but rather as absolute need, a need which is simultaneously absolutely selfless yet committed to human interests. Only such a need can be content with difference to which it is necessary to remain **in**-different.

Moral Law Cannot be Represented

The subject of free will exists and is created in the difference between Reason and Understanding, as a consequence of free causality. Free causality is the difference between existence and creation. The subject of free will forms maxims which always already fail their object, owing to the sacrificial relationship between Reason and Understanding. Hence, the subject of free will is dependent upon the failure of representation and (or as) sacrifice. This gives the maxim known as **the categorical imperative**.

The categorical imperative implies that the subject must act according to the idea of the moral law, even though this law cannot be represented.

The purpose of the *Critique of Practical Reason*, as critique, is to guard against the desire to unify representation (Understanding) and freedom (Reason), so as to retain a sense of difference between the two faculties, despite the fact that they are inextricably linked.

Kant's Physical Obsessions

Kant was fanatically preoccupied with physical health, both his own and that of others. He seems to have abhorred bodily fluids and took great pains never to sweat. One of his biographers has noted that, "Even in the most sultry summer night, if the slightest trace of perspiration had sullied his night-dress, he spoke of it with emphasis, as of an accident that perfectly shocked him".

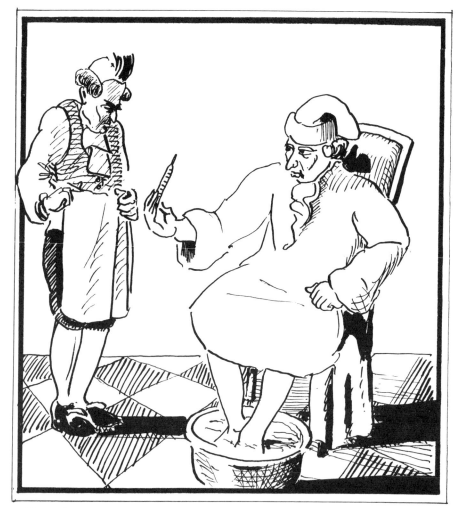

Kant's bedroom was never heated, even in the coldest weather; but his study was kept at 75 degrees Fahrenheit in all seasons. A contemporary once described his physical appearance as "drier than dust . . . His person was small; and possibly a more meagre, arid, parched anatomy of a man has not appeared upon this earth".

Kant developed a technique of breathing only through his nose, night and day, because he believed only in this way could he get rid of catarrh and cough. As a consequence of his method of breathing, he refused to take a companion on his daily walk in case conversation forced him to breathe through his mouth whilst in the open air.

The *Critique of Judgement* (1790)

Having investigated judgements concerning knowledge (first *Critique*) and morality (second *Critique*), Kant turns to the **power of judgement** itself. The third *Critique* affirms that judgement is a universal power, to which everyone is bound. As such, judgement is not simply a power of discrimination or selection. It exceeds these processes either through the possibility for accord (the beautiful) or sacrifice (the sublime).

*My final **Critique** attempts to locate a higher form of feeling in an aesthetic judgement, which can be said to determine **a priori** experiences of pleasure and pain. These experiences are indicative of the harmony or sacrifice involved in judgement.*

Aesthetic judgements, or *judgements of taste*, are explored in relation to the beautiful and the sublime respectively.

In the section entitled "Dialectic of Taste", Kant sets out the **antinomy of taste**.

Thesis: A judgement of taste is not based on concepts; for otherwise one could dispute about it and decide by means of proofs.

Antithesis: A judgement of taste is based on concepts; otherwise one could not lay claim to other people's assent.

The reasoning behind this resolution is laid out in the sections on the analytic of the beautiful and the sublime.

Analytic of the Beautiful

For Kant, judgements of the beautiful are not about "the agreeableness or disagreeableness" of a sensation. They are not reducible to the question of enjoyment, which is "a passive pleasure, conditioned pathologically by stimuli". Enjoyment is always a matter of subjective and individual taste, and cannot be aligned with a universal feeling.

This applies, for instance, to the smell of a flower. We cannot be certain whether a person is getting the very same sensation as we are getting.

Sensual enjoyment depends upon discernment, which is an associative and comparative sense. This is at work in the enjoyment of "the green colour of meadows", or in "the tone of a violin". It is also why "foliage" is enjoyed, by extracting pleasure from "flowers, free designs and lines aimlessly intertwined".

Judgement and Feeling

Several operations occur for a judgement of the beautiful to arise. As in the first *Critique*, Imagination intuits and presents data (space and time) to Understanding. But in contrast to the first *Critique*, Understanding does not convert this intuition into a search for predication via the categories. This is because a non-cognitive feeling accompanies the intuition, which substitutes for the need to utilize the categories.

Judgement and Form

Judgements of the beautiful depend on **form** "undisturbed and uninterrupted by any sensation". This process of *forming* involves Imagination and Understanding. Imagination presents the form (of Nature) to Understanding, for which no determinate concept can be formed. That which is presented to Understanding conforms simply to its "power" to form concepts, i.e., a power to form consciousness, despite the fact that there is nothing to be conscious of.

This gives rise to a **disinterested** judgement of taste regarding the beautiful.

*It is merely **contemplative**, not a cognitive judgement (whether theoretical or practical) and hence is neither **based** on concepts, nor directed to them as **purposes**.*

Kant's concept of "disinterestedness" has often been misinterpreted. What does he mean by it – and how does he arrive at it?

The Unknown in its Relation to Judgement

The feeling of disinterested judgement is fundamentally different from other types of feelings with their own particular interests (such as the legislative operations of Understanding *interested* in speculative knowledge, and of Reason *interested* in practical desire).

Whereas the first and second *Critiques* were dedicated to confirming that something happens that is beyond the knowledge and desire of the subject, the third *Critique* affirms the unknown (or the not knowing – the failure of Understanding to form concepts).

Kant suggests that the unknown requires absolutely no representation. Therefore, the unknown is not opposed, or dialectically related to, an implied presence as in metaphysics.

Kant attempts to figure **nothingness** as problematical – rather than as mere "absence" – through a sense of process outside of any concept.

The Place of Feeling in Judgement

Feeling intervenes between Imagination and Understanding. Feeling defers, and even prevents, Understanding from applying the categories, such that no *principle* of predication can be developed from this feeling. Ideas of truth, decency or justice are therefore inoperative.

However, whilst such judgements do not apply to the concepts themselves, they are indicative of Understanding's *power to form concepts*.

The Sensuality of Thought

Kant is not concerned to discover an essence of the beautiful, nor does he wish to prescribe the experience of beauty by relating it to particular attributes of objects or people.

Rather, he suggests that the beautiful prompts Understanding into speculation. The beautiful is, therefore, pure feeling. But, as such, it is also the *pleasure of thought*.

The pleasure we take in the beautiful is a pleasure which accompanies our ordinary apprehension of an object by means of the Imagination (our power of intuition) in relation to the Understanding (our power of concepts).

Thought possesses its own sensuality which separates Understanding from Imagination. But this means that Understanding no longer dominates Imagination. Understanding *creates* feeling, rather than simply receives and transforms it. This guarantees that the two faculties can operate in harmony, and amounts to a universal judgement of taste.

We must be entitled to assume **a priori** that a presentation's harmony with these conditions of the power of judgement is valid for everyone.

From this there follows Kant's idea of a *sensus communis*. This is "the idea of a sense shared" by everyone.

The Priority of Design

Kant's ideas of what constitutes the "form" of aesthetic judgement were undoubtedly shaped by historically- and culturally-conditioned opinions. He states that colours and sounds do not define the "form" of Nature: these are merely "charms" which supplement and "enliven the presentation".

Kant repeats an opposition between the sensual and intellectual aspects of art which had been debated since at least the 17th century amongst patrons and artists in Italy – the debate concerning *colore* (colour) and *disegno* (design).

Peter Paul Rubens (1577–1640) represented the colour tendency and **Nicolas Poussin** (1594–1665) the design.

Nature Versus Artifice

Kant states that judgements concerning the beautiful can only be made in relation to Nature. Hence, his dictum that he who leaves a museum to turn towards the beauties of Nature deserves respect. Artifice, for Kant, is a form of deceit. "We have cases where some jovial innkeeper plays a trick on the guests, hiding in a bush some roguish youngster who (with a reed or rush in his mouth) knows how to copy the nightingale's song in a way very similar to Nature's. But as soon as one realizes that it is all deception, no one will long endure listening to this song that before he had considered so charming."

But Nature tends to conceal its beauty, and art is required to lend it a sense of design and purpose. This can only be achieved through fine art.

Nature, Design and Ornament

Kant's prejudice against artifice is not entire. Indeed, he locates the notion of design not in relation to Nature but the visual arts, including painting, sculpture, architecture, dance and horticulture. Design "is either play of shapes (in space, namely mimetic art and dance), or mere play of sensations (in time)".

*But even in art, design is always already extrinsic to the object. It is also that which gives a paradoxical essence to the supplement or **parergon**.*

"Even what we call ornaments (*parerga*), i.e., what does not belong to the whole presentation of the object as an intrinsic constituent, but [is] only an extrinsic addition, does indeed increase our taste's liking, and yet it too does so only by its form, as in the case of picture frames, or drapery on statues, or colonnades around magnificent buildings."

Genius Transforms Nature

Nature seems to conceal its own design. "How are we to explain why Nature has so extravagantly spread beauty everywhere, even at the bottom of the ocean?"

The means by which Kant attempts to unite the contradiction between form in Nature and art is through the figure of the **genius**. In other words, the genius is the catalyst by which Nature can be seen to *trans*-form itself into art.

The genius is a fine artist. The fine arts are distinguished from crafts (e.g. watchmaking and smith-making) as well as from the "agreeable arts" (e.g. "the art of furnishing a table", "telling stories entertainingly", "using jest and laughter to induce a certain cheerful tone").

The Order of the Arts

For Kant, the principal fine arts are, in order of priority: poetry, oratory, music, painting. Poetry "holds the highest rank since it fortifies the mind: for it lets the mind feel its ability – free, spontaneous, and independent of natural determination – to contemplate and judge phenomenal Nature".

Romantic Ideas of Genius

Kant repeats a number of characteristically Romantic ideas about genius and its origins in metaphysical notions of the divine. However, by the 18th century, the source of genius was seen to arise less from divine favour than from the bounty of Nature, as a kind of birthright.

*The term **genius** is derived from the Latin word meaning the guardian and guiding spirit that each person is given as his own at birth, and to whose inspiration his original ideas are due.*

Kant's genius is a male whose work is absolutely original, expressive of an innate, animating "spirit" (*Geist*). The genius breaks with tradition by not following rules or prescriptions. Owing to its exemplary character, the art of the genius is destined to be copied by others and even to found schools of followers and adherents. However, it can only be truly understood or appreciated by another genius, to whom it is addressed. The product of a genius is meant not to be imitated, but to be followed by another genius.

Genius and Deformation

Kant's analysis of genius is more complex and far-reaching than typical Romantic views on the subject. Kant refers to the "deformity" inherent in the art of genius as a consequence of the way in which genius reveals that illusion *is* reality.

Why do you say "deformity"?

Because, in a sense, reality cannot be known.

Imagination is sacrificed to, or *de*-formed by, Understanding. Only the form in which concepts take shape survives. To put it another way, Nature de-forms or sacrifices itself in order to *become* art. Art represents this sacrifice, yet it does not understand it. Hence, art is salvation, a residue of sacrifice and form.

Genius represents that which is always already absent ("the object"). This applies both to "ideas of invisible beings, the realm of the blessed, the realm of hell, eternity, creation", as well as to "death, envy, and all the other vices, as well as love, fame, and so on".

"Genius is the innate mental predisposition (*ingenium*) through which Nature gives the rule to art."

Genius exists both within and as the difference between infinity (Nature) and finitude (art). As such, genius is a force rather than the attribute of an individual subject. It is a conduit that realizes an impersonal and unconscious process.

If an author owes a product to his genius, he himself does not know how he came by the ideas for it; nor is it in his power to devise such products at his pleasure, or by following a plan, nor to communicate his procedure to others in precepts that would enable them to bring about like products.

Analytic of the Sublime

Judgements of taste concerning the beautiful do not bring the faculty of Reason into play, and therefore only stand as a sign of the "good". Judgements of taste concerning the sublime are different in this respect: they are inextricably bound up with Reason's idea of freedom.

The Greek author **Longinus** was the first writer to treat the sublime in relation to aesthetics (i.e. questions of sensation). His treatise *On the Sublime* was written in the middle of the 1st century A.D. The French critic **Nicolas Boileau** (1636–1711) revived the question of the sublime, and also translated Longinus' text.

Like Longinus, I considered the sublime to be the lofty style in rhetoric and poetry.

In the 17th and 18th centuries, the sublime became associated with wildness and vastness in Nature, and any phenomena which gave rise to a sense of chaos.

Burke's View of the Sublime

Kant's theory of the sublime was partly formed in response to a text by the English politician **Edmund Burke** (1729–97), entitled ***Philosophical Enquiry Into the Origin of Our Ideas of the Sublime and Beautiful*** (1757). For Burke, *delight* – or the negative pleasure which characterizes the feeling of the sublime – arises from the removal of the threat of pain. Certain objects and sensations pose a threat to self-preservation: shadows, solitude, silence, and the approach of death announce the extinction of communication and life.

Burke attributed to poetry the two-fold function of inspiring terror (the threat of language's cessation), and of meeting the challenge posed by this failure of the word by provoking "the advent of an 'unheard of' phrase". A simple expression like "The Angel of the Lord" opens up an infinite number of associations for the mind.

The Mathematical Sublime

Kant first wrote on the subject of the sublime in 1764, in ***Observations on the Feeling of the Beautiful and the Sublime***. There, he contrasted the feeling of the beautiful to the sublime. "The sublime *moves*, whilst the beautiful *charms*." In the *Critique of Judgement*, Kant states that the experience of the sublime arises through an excess of sensory information.

There are two ways in which such an experience may occur. Either through

This amounts to an experience of formlessness.

an overwhelming sensation of immensity or of power: "the mathematical sublime" and "the dynamic sublime".

The mathematical sublime is attendant upon feelings of bewilderment or perplexity as when, for instance, first entering St Peter's in Rome or standing close to a monumental edifice such as the Pyramids. In the case of the Pyramids, "the eye needs some time to complete the apprehension from the base to the peak, but during that time some of the earlier parts are invariably extinguished in the Imagination before it has apprehended the later ones, and hence the comprehension is never complete".

The Dynamic Sublime

In the dynamic sublime, formless experience occurs through interaction with "Nature as a might": "bold, overhanging and, as it were, threatening rocks, thunderclouds piling up in the sky and moving about accompanied by lightning and thunderclaps, volcanoes with all their destructive power, hurricanes with all the devastation they leave behind, the boundless ocean heaved up, the high waterfall of a mighty river . . ."

These phenomena arouse a feeling of terror and a sense of abject inferiority. But other feelings ensue as a counter-force, indicating a condition of "free judgement". Thus, "a virtuous person fears God without being afraid of him", and a great warrior will demonstrate "all the virtues of peace – gentleness, sympathy, and even appropriate care for his own person – precisely because they reveal . . . that his mind cannot be subdued by danger".

Experiencing the Sublime

Kant insists that the experience of the sublime is not dependent upon the object (e.g. Nature), but on the subject. The Savoyard peasant understood this well when he called "anyone a fool who fancies glaciered mountains".

For this reason, Kant fully accords with the prohibition upon images

advocated in the book of *Exodus*. "Perhaps the most sublime passage in the Jewish Law is the commandment: 'Thou shalt not make unto thee any graven image, or any likeness of any thing that is in heaven or on earth, or under the earth', etc . . . This pure, elevating, and merely negative exhibition of morality involves no danger of fanaticism, which is *the delusion of wanting to **see** something beyond all bounds of sensibility.*"

Experience of the sublime is engendered by the faculty of Imagination. This build-up of sensory stimuli in Imagination prevents Understanding from functioning. Initially, this leads to a feeling of displeasure and pain. The build-up of sensation in Imagination originates in the difference between the experience of three elements: the immensity or power associated with the *object* (e.g. Nature), or with *infinity* and *freedom*.

The experience of vastness or power is not the same as an experience of infinity. Nor are they simply analogous to each other, yet they are not entirely different.

The instability of the relationship between these two experiences gives rise to the initial feeling of displeasure or pain that is attendant upon the sublime. This signals the "sacrifice of Imagination".

Excess of Freedom

But displeasure and pain are followed by pleasure. The instability between the relationship of Nature and infinity demonstrates an excess. And this excess is freedom: the presence of Reason.

Whilst the greatest power of sensibility (Imagination) is inadequate, it is in harmony with rational ideas (Reason), insofar as striving towards them is still a law for us.

As a consequence, "Imagination acquires an expansion and a might that surpasses the one it sacrifices".

Although it is in the nature of the experience that Imagination can never identify with Reason and the idea of freedom, "the basis of this might is concealed from it; instead the Imagination feels the sacrifice or deprivation and at the same time the cause to which it is being subjugated".

Thus, Imagination and Reason confront each other in a relation of discord, wherein Imagination is continually subjected by Reason to the idea that it cannot grasp freedom.

But this provokes further the experience of the sublime, resulting in "an exhibition of the infinite". Such exhibition "can never be more than merely negative", since it always involves the sacrifice of Imagination to Reason and the idea of freedom.

Freedom From Nature

Freedom's intervention guarantees that Man dominates Nature, rather than vice versa. But Nature does not present itself spontaneously. Hence, what precedes convention and society for Kant is not Nature but "culture".

The fact that a judgement about the sublime in Nature requires culture . . . still in no way implies that it was initially produced by culture and then introduced to society by way of (say) mere convention. Rather, it has its foundation in human nature: in something that, along with common sense, we may require and demand of everyone.

"Thus any spectator who beholds massive mountains climbing skyward, deep gorges with raging streams in them, wastelands lying in deep shadow and inviting melancholy meditation and so on, is seized by *amazement* bordering on terror, by horror and a sacred thrill. But since he knows he is safe, this is not actual fear: it is merely our attempt to incur it with our Imagination, in order that we may feel that very power's might and connect the mental agitation this arouses with the mind's state of rest. In this way we feel our superiority to Nature within ourselves, and hence also to Nature outside us insofar as it can influence our feeling of well-being."

Freedom, Pain and Desire

The experience of freedom is shattering, always preceded and bounded by pain (and dependent upon pain). Yet this affirms the subject's uniqueness to experience freedom. Pain is the sense of a division or a difference between the subject and the infinite (between life and death), an experience of Nature's utter *in*-difference. Such an absolute experience of Nature's implacability is an experience of desire for that which is beyond experience (the Other). This is to experience desire absolutely, since the Other is absolutely absent: sacrifice as desire, desire as sacrifice.

Critique of Teleological Judgement

All judgements of taste refer to a "purposiveness without purpose" in Nature, meaning that the question of predication is exceeded by a *sense* of purpose. It is no longer a matter of asking upon what basis knowledge or morality exists, since feeling produces and supplants this question.

In the final section of the *Critique of Judgement*, entitled "Critique of Teleological Judgement", Kant explores the implications of his previous inquiry for scientific and religious ideas of purpose.

Both science and religion share a desire to ascribe a cause to an effect. Religion constantly demands, "Why does Man exist?". And, in asking this question, implies that the question is with purpose even though it might not necessarily be answered. Mechanistic science, in creating functional models for the laws of motion, suggests that there are underlying principles to Nature.

The aim of the "Critique of Teleological Judgement" is to guard against the error of confusing *purpose* with *intentionality*. Kant allows, for instance, that grass is there for sheep and cattle, and dreams exist to keep the Imagination in play. But this does not mean that they were created *intentionally*.

Disregarding intention means that Kant affirms the arbitrary and the unexpected. They exist on account of experience. He offers the maxim, "Everything in the world is good for something or other; nothing in it is gratuitous; everything is purposive in relation to the whole".

Kant refutes the thesis that the goal of the human race is happiness. Culture is the ultimate aim pursued by Nature in the human race. It makes Man more "receptive to ideas" and is the condition for thinking the unconditioned (freedom).

"To produce in a rational being the general aptitude for the aims which please him (and consequently in his freedom), that is culture."

Kant and Religion

Kant's views on religion in the last decade of his active career reflect the ideas developed in the three *Critiques*.

Christian worship is of no more importance than any other form of religious worship.

"Whether the hypocrite makes his legalistic visit to church or a pilgrimage to the shrines of Loretto or Palestine, whether he brings his prayer formulas to the heavenly authorities by his lips or, like the Tibetan . . . does it by a prayer wheel, or whatever kind of surrogate for the moral service of God it may be, it is all worth just the same." (***Religion Within the Limits of Reason Alone***, 1793)

For Kant, the servile worship of God was no substitute for a "transcendental critique". As a consequence, he states that morality "in no way needs religion for its own service (objectively, as regards willing, as well as subjectively, as regards ability), but in virtue of pure practical Reason it is sufficient unto itself".

The Biblical figure of Job came to stand for Kant as the forerunner of Enlightenment thinking.

Job disclaimed the right to represent God's motives and wishes, and criticized others for attempting to do so.

Job, An Enlightenment Figure

"Job speaks the way he thinks and the way he is expected to, and speaks as probably every man in his situation would be expected to do; his friends speak in the opposite way, as if they were being covertly overheard by the Mighty One, whom they are justifying, and to stand in whose favour is, in their judgement, dearer than to be truthful."

"Job would most probably have experienced a nasty fate at the hands of any tribunal of dogmatic theologians, a synod, an inquisition, a pack of reverends, or any consistory of our day." (***On the Failure of All Philosophical Attempts at Theodicy***, 1791)

What is Enlightenment?

In the 1790s, Kant's ideas came into conflict with the state authorities. Kant had prepared for this event in an article of 1784. Published in the journal *Berlinische Monatsschrift*, it was written as a response to a question set by the editors: "*What is Enlightenment?*".

In this text, Kant defines Enlightenment as an "exit" or "way out" (*Ausgang*), but this is conceived of in a negative way as a (continuous) refusal of prescriptive forms of authority. Enlightenment bears a *Wahlspruch* (literally, a heraldic device, but metaphorically a motto or instruction).

This is in contrast to the state of humanity in its immaturity in which the prescription runs: "Don't think, just follow orders."

Private and Public Reason

Kant attempts to safeguard Enlightenment's imperative by drawing a distinction between the private and public use of Reason. The private use of Reason is exercised when Man is "a cog in the machine", that is, when performing a role in society as a soldier, taxpayer, pastor or civil servant. Thus, in the private sphere, Man is placed in a circumscribed position, where he has to apply particular rules and pursue particular ends.

As a consequence of these responsibilities, Kant provides the motto for humanity in its mature state: "Obey, and you will be able to reason as much as you like."

Kant's conclusion to the article exceeds these diplomatic manoeuvres by proposing to King Frederick William II, in scarcely veiled terms, a contract.

In 1794 Kant published his article, "The End of all Things", in the *Berlinische Monatsschrift*, in which he predicted an end to morality (hence the title of the article) if free-thinking within Christianity were to be obstructed by an intransigent authority. "Should it once happen that Christianity stops being lovable (which could indeed occur were it armed with imperious authority, instead of its gentle spirit), then rejection and rebellion against it would inevitably come to be the dominant way of thought among men."

A Royal Warning

On 1 October 1794, Kant was sent a letter, signed by the King, in which he was reproached for having "misused" his philosophy "for the distortion and debasing of many principal and basic teachings of Holy Scripture and of Christianity", and in which he was instructed to avoid the Royal disfavour and to be guilty of nothing similar, "otherwise you can unfailingly expect, on continued recalcitrance, unpleasant consequences".

In writing his defence, Kant made recourse to his previous arguments concerning the private and public use of Reason. He rejected the accusation that he had made any judgement on the Bible and Christianity in his teaching.

Nevertheless, Kant undertook not to discuss religious matters in public again.

Although religion was prohibited from discussion, Kant continued to publish works about the state and the question of rights and freedom: **Perpetual Peace**, 1795; **The Metaphysics of Morals**, 1797; and **The Conflict of the Faculties**, 1798, which refers to the French Revolution. Ultimately, Kant does not necessarily support either the Royalists or the Republicans.

What concerns me is that the concept of freedom is at stake in the events of the revolution.

"I maintain that this revolution has aroused in the hearts and desires of all spectators who are not themselves caught up in it a sympathy which borders almost on enthusiasm . . . It cannot therefore have been caused by anything other than a moral disposition within the human race."

Kant's Last Days

Detailed information survives of the period preceding Kant's death. This was recorded by his friends and earliest biographers, Pastor Wasianski and Ludwig Ernst Borowski. The information provided by these biographers was later collated by **Thomas de Quincey** (1785–1859) and published as an article in the early 19th century, entitled "The Last Days of Immanuel Kant".

Kant developed cerebral arteriosclerosis. His memory for recent events began to fail, although he continued to recall remote events with accuracy, and could repeat long passages of poetry, especially from Virgil's *Aeneid*. He also developed strange delusions about electricity.

He lost all accurate measurement of time, and became impatient with his servants. In 1802, Kant dismissed his long-serving valet, Lampe. The reason for this remains obscure, although there are possible grounds to believe that the cause was sexual harassment!

In his diary for February 1802, Kant wrote: "The name of Lampe must now be remembered no more."

As the winter of 1802–3 approached, Kant complained of stomach aches. He had difficulty in sleeping and was terrified by his dreams. In the spring of 1803 he began to lose his appetite; soon after, his sight also started to deteriorate. On occasions, he was still capable of responding to questions on matters of philosophy and science. But gradually, he became unable to communicate with others or even to recognize them.

He died on 12 February 1804, just two months before his eightieth birthday. His fame ensured a public funeral in the cathedral at Königsberg, attended by dignitaries from all over Prussia.

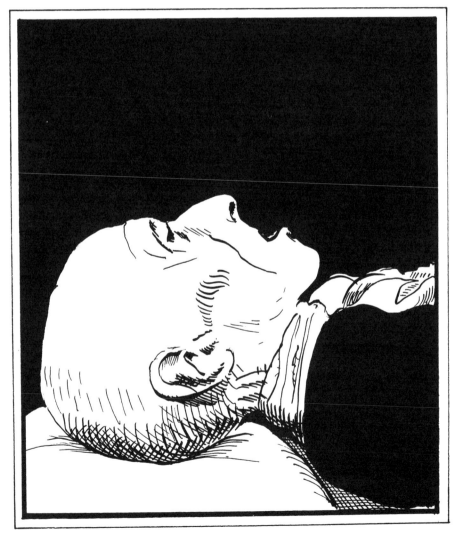

AFTER KANT

Introduction

The contemporary philosopher **Jean-François Lyotard** (b. 1924) writes, "The name Kant marks at once the prologue and epilogue to modernity. And as epilogue to modernity, it is also a prologue to postmodernity." (*The Sign of History*, 1982)

As Lyotard suggests, Kant's philosophical legacy is perhaps best understood and negotiated as that which borders upon different historical eras. It marks out modernity's philosophical directions and concerns – without necessarily over-determining them – whilst it crosses into a further epoch.

This does not imply that Kant's philosophy will be realized or fulfilled by postmodernity. Rather, it is in the nature of such a philosophy to engender conceptual change and revaluation which is in excess of narratives of historical advance and progress.

What follows is a series of sketches of some of the major modern and postmodern philosophers whose work may be seen to be involved in such a revaluation. These pages are offered only as clues which, it is hoped, will help the reader to see how later philosophers have gained from the continuing relevance and power of Kant's criticism of philosophy.

Georg Wilhelm Friedrich Hegel (1770–1831)

Following Kant, Hegel asserts that the supreme demand of the modern age is that thought derive all its knowledge and values freely and autonomously through Reason. Furthermore, Reason should not make any unwarranted assumptions about itself. However, Hegel's search for a "science of logic" without presuppositions led him to doubt that Kant's organization of the categories was adequate to thought.

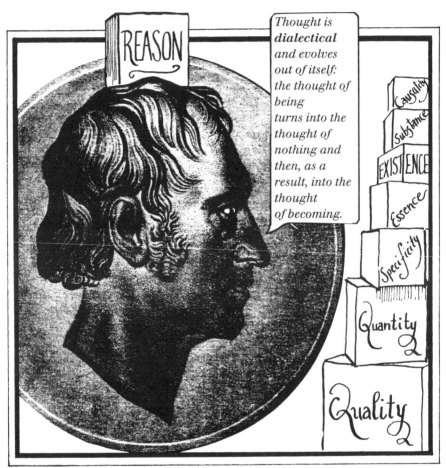

Thought is *dialectical* and evolves out of itself: the thought of being turns into the thought of nothing and then, as a result, into the thought of becoming.

Since to think *being* is also to think *becoming*, Hegel arranges the categories of thought in a sequential order: quality, quantity, specificity, essence and existence, substance and causality, followed ultimately by self-determining Reason. From this Hegel derives a method of immanent development and criticism, in which each category reveals the truth in terms of both potential and limit of the previous determination in ascending order. This principle is "the soul of all truly scientific knowledge".

Like Kant, Hegel believes that the truly free will is "the will that wills itself and its own freedom". Hegel establishes a philosophy of rights, in contrast to a philosophy of duty, which, in his view, does not preclude violations such as theft and murder. In his **Philosophy of Right** (1821), Hegel declares: "The absolute right is the right to have rights." From this he derives the imperative: "Be a person and respect others as persons."

As with Kant, aesthetics is a crucial component of Hegel's philosophy. Art, along with religion (specifically Christianity) and philosophy, unifies and reconciles opposites, and in so doing reveals the truth ("Idea").

Art is the sensuous appearance of the Idea, a heightened shining of things.

In certain forms of art the Idea is given in its absence and through indeterminate qualities. Hegel cites *Macbeth* where the Idea – Macbeth's strength of character – emerges in spite of his superstition and vulnerability. Hegel especially admired Greek sculpture, but he also valued the realist tradition in art (e.g. Murillo's paintings of beggar boys) which he argued rendered freedom visible.

Friedrich Nietzsche (1844–1900)

Nietzsche declared his philosophy to consist of "a revaluation of all values". Specifically, this entailed the destruction, or "overcoming", of Christian and metaphysical values. Nietzsche believed such values were "hostile to life", since they fostered an unnecessary fear of the contradictions inherent to **power**.

To Nietzsche, Kant is "a cunning Christian", desperate to hang on to the last vestiges of metaphysics. The noumenon is a concept of transcendental immanence, substituting for religious faith. The categorical imperative leads "back to God" by reasserting a sense of obligation.

But there is another side to Kant for Nietzsche.

Kant's scepticism engenders a critical account of knowledge and freedom which inevitably leads to the overthrow of metaphysics.

Kant is likened to "a fox who loses his way and strays back into his cage". Although Nietzsche grants that "it had been his strength and cleverness that had broken open the cage!".

What does power mean for Nietzsche? It resides in two tendencies. The ability continually to stimulate demands from others and to respond to them. This is why, in Nietzsche's view, "the artist gives rather than receives". But it also consists of the capacity to relinquish the loved object when creativity is threatened, such that guilt is imputed to the one who renounces rather than the rejected party. This is a necessary part of the "battle of the sexes" or human relations.

These ideas find no exact replication in Kant's philosophy. Indeed, as Nietzsche implies, they are expressly designed to depart from Kant's underlying metaphysics. And yet Kant's analysis of judgement in relation to aesthetics as a matter of sensation (third *Critique*) may be seen to anticipate Nietzsche's analysis of power after "the death of God" in terms of conflictual emotions coupled to expenditures of energies.

Similarly, both thinkers use the figure of the genius to explore their ideas. For Kant, the genius' powers are formed by unconscious drives; likewise in Nietzsche they are created by, and from, feelings which exceed the subject's limits: "An excitation of the animal functions through the images and desires of intensified life." (***The Will to Power***, 1887)

Martin Heidegger (1889–1976)

Heidegger's central concern is with the question of Being (ontology), but also the possibility that this question may cease to have importance through the remembering of its history. Heidegger believed that Kant's philosophy revolved around the major problematic which he was also concerned with, that of *Dasein* ("to be there"). This refers to the place where being develops and can be reached.

Heidegger is excited by Kant's suggestion that the "thing in itself" is not different from the appearance, but merely the same thing viewed under a different light.

*I interpret this as meaning that the "thing in itself" does not lie above or beyond appearances, as is suggested in certain traditions of metaphysics. Rather the "thing in itself" remains concealed because its own appearance **is** concealment. But what is revealed is our ability to **see** this.*

This means that the "thing in itself" is not separable from finite consciousness.

Heidegger draws attention to the significance of this deduction by asking how knowledge of the "thing in itself" can be given. "How can a finite being which as such is delivered up to the essence and is dependent on its reception have knowledge of, i.e., intuit, the essent before it is given without being its creator?" (**Kant and the Problem of Metaphysics**, 1930). This is Heidegger's reformulation of Kant's question of the *a priori* synthetic judgement.

For Heidegger, the problem of knowledge is always repeated.

*Repetition is a process of **dis**-closure, endlessly unearthing and revealing, remembering and forgetting the finite possibilities of the knowledge of being.*

Such a process is the very means by which the question of **being** discovers its "primordial" links with the question of **time**. These ideas are expounded in Heidegger's great work, **Being and Time** (1927).

Michel Foucault (1926–84)

Foucault's primary concern is to define the present historical condition. This is summarized in the question: "What difference does today introduce with respect to yesterday?"

Foucault's historico-critical investigations cover a wide range of topics: sanity and insanity, sickness and health, crime and the law, the role of sexual relations. These investigations are tied together by an overriding interest in what Foucault calls **power/knowledge**. Historically concrete human experience is defined in terms of discourses, which function through a normative collection of rules . . .

For instance, rules which operate in distinguishing the permitted and the forbidden or the normal and the pathological.

. . . and by means of a mode of relation to oneself.

For Foucault, Kant's essay *What is Enlightenment?* identifies important issues at stake in his own work, particularly in the way that questions of philosophy and modernity intersect.

Foucault concurs with Kant's suggestion that modernity should be characterized in terms of an *attitude* which depends upon an interaction between the private and public uses of Reason. For Foucault, this relationship between private and public Reason is specifically a political problem, in which the duties and responsibilities of the subject are offered for critique. But the process of critique does not divide the state from the individual, or the employer from the employee.

*Enlightenment implies a contract which obliges **all** parties to allow inquiry into the limits pertaining to the understanding of a designated work or activity.*

Foucault defines critique as "a permanent creation of ourselves in our autonomy". The aim of modernity is to instil *change*, both from within and for itself. "We separate out, from the contingency that has made us what we are, the possibility of no longer being, doing, or thinking what we are, do, or think." To implement this separation is to create what Foucault calls "the undefined work of freedom".

Jean-François Lyotard (b. 1924)

The underlying concerns of Lyotard's philosophy lie in two Kantian questions, those of **foundations** (upon what are knowledge and ethics predicated?) and **freedom**. Lyotard provides a critique of the "meta-narratives" of modernity: the idea that knowledge is produced for its own sake (e.g. Hegel), and the idea that knowledge is produced with the aim of achieving freedom (e.g. Marx).

Lyotard concurs with Kant's dictum that "philosophy cannot be learned: at most one can learn to *philosophize*". Judgement, therefore, remains the key issue and points to the *question* of how to represent the historical totality.

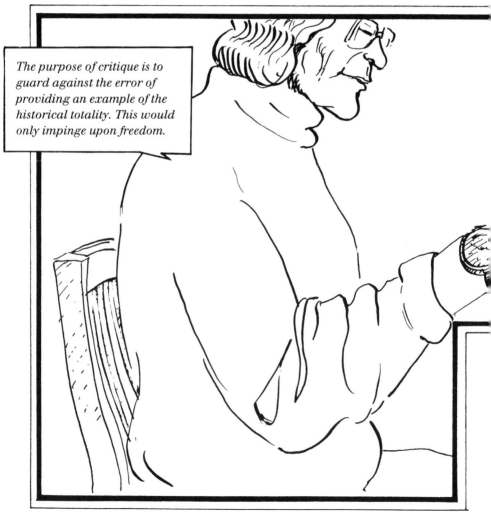

The purpose of critique is to guard against the error of providing an example of the historical totality. This would only impinge upon freedom.

As Kant suggested, with knowledge subject to its own limits, there are no immutable principles for ethical behaviour.

The only option left is to affirm that the pain of freedom and responsibility is bound up with the experience of injustice.

These indeterminate feelings are associated with the **sublime** (freedom), an interruptive force acting from within and upon knowledge. "Progress" then becomes the possibility of affirming the heterogeneity and unpredictability of discourse as the corollary of the sublime as interruptive force.

Art may be a power capable of representing such an event. "Art is not a genre defined in terms of an end (the pleasure of the addressee) and still less is it a game whose rules have to be discovered. It must constantly testify to the occurrence by letting the occurrence be."

Jacques Derrida (b. 1930)

Derrida approaches the issues of ontology and epistemology (questions of Being and knowledge respectively) via the supplementary question of **writing** as a philosophical activity and concern. He states that "there is nothing outside the text", thus drawing attention to the absence of representation's limits. From this there follows the Kantian-derived question: how does recognition of the absence of limits take place?

Derrida observes that concepts of subjectivity and identity are traditionally structured in terms of hierarchically organized binary oppositions: active – passive, plenitude – lack, inside – outside, speech – writing, etc.

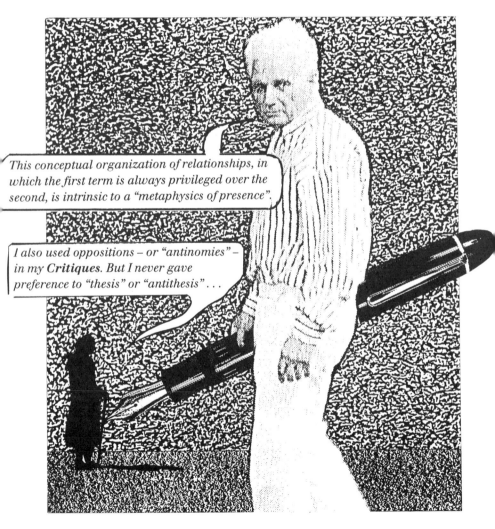

This conceptual organization of relationships, in which the first term is always privileged over the second, is intrinsic to a "metaphysics of presence".

*I also used oppositions – or "antinomies" – in my **Critiques**. But I never gave preference to "thesis" or "antithesis" . . .*

In contrast to these ideas, Derrida's philosophy consists of **deconstructions**. The plurality of the term is intended to safeguard "the heterogeneity and the multiplicity, the necessary multiplicity of gestures, of fields, of styles. Deconstruction is not a system, not a method, it cannot be homogenized".

In Derrida's view, the modern tradition of philosophy is composed of ruptures and mutations repeated throughout history.

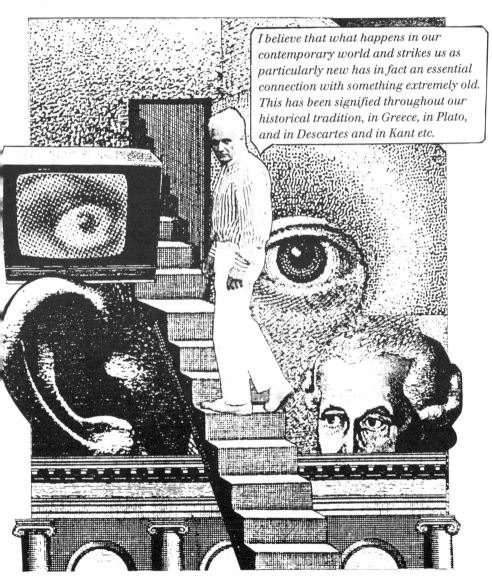

I believe that what happens in our contemporary world and strikes us as particularly new has in fact an essential connection with something extremely old. This has been signified throughout our historical tradition, in Greece, in Plato, and in Descartes and in Kant etc.

Derrida's analysis of Kant's *Critique of Judgement* (**The Truth in Painting**, 1978) concentrates on the idea of the supplement or "parergon".

Derrida shows that the supplement is not simply the repressed term within a binary structure, e.g. painting vs. frame. Rather, it is that which is always already **absent** as a condition of the structure itself. This "deconstructs" the possibility of a mutual relation between binary terms and undermines the structure itself.

According to Derrida, inconsistencies in the *Critique of Judgement* develop as a consequence of Kant's fantasy that to obtain the truth is to achieve the **end** of writing. But Derrida's aim is not simply to fault Kant or his arguments. Rather the – inevitable – appearance of these inconsistencies informs Derrida's own text and so becomes a matter for affirming the fallibility of the subject as the proponent of writing's ends.

Although the decorations on the framing devices – the "parerga" – are included within the orbit of judgements of beauty, the idea is maintained that pictures and architecture are separable from their frames.

Conclusion

The philosophical legacy which passes from Kant to today through the critical engagement of contemporary thinkers is not staged for the sake of "enlightenment" in its universalist progressive sense. Rather, the complexities of consciousness, recognition and memory, upon which these post-Kantian philosophers reflect, imply that we cannot attain salvation from ourselves as metaphysics had envisaged.

Philosophy continues Kant's autonomous and self-critical investigation through its own misapprehensions. This "project" is guaranteed in the absence of any exemplary model or standard by which to reproduce the truth: as Derrida says, "there is nothing outside the text".

Kant himself hoped to set philosophy on the footing of a science. But this was not meant ultimately in its humanist sense, as a science of empirically or logically derived precepts or facts. Rather it was intended as an affirmation, in the most systematic terms possible, of a philosophy which derived its meanings from its own limits and fallibility. As such, it was intended to counter the programmatic concerns of culture and politics – or indeed any organization intent upon establishing itself in the name of prescribed knowledges or morals. In Kant's hands, philosophy became an implosive science of critique: "The love which the reasonable being has for the supreme ends of human reason."

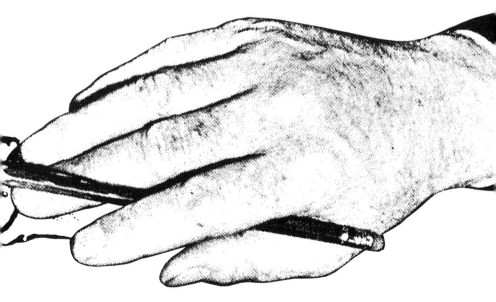

Further Reading

Kant's Life

Details of Kant's life originate principally from the reminiscences of several of his friends – Ludwig Borowski, Reinhold Jachmann, F.T. Rink and Pastor E.A.C. Wasianski. Many of these details were collated later in the 19th century by the English Romantic writer Thomas de Quincey in his fascinating portrayal of Kant in his old age as a Lear-like figure ("The Last Days of Immanuel Kant", in *The Works of Thomas de Quincey*, A. & C. Black, 16 vols., Edinburgh 1862–83, vol. 4, available in specialist libraries only). Most books on Kant's life incorporate studies of his philosophy. Ernst Cassirer's *Kant's Life and Thought* (tr. James Haden, Yale University Press, London & New Haven, Conn. 1981) was a path-finding book in its time (originally published 1918). Arsenij Gulyga's *Immanuel Kant: His Life and Thought* (tr. Marijan Despalatovic, Birkhauser Inc., Boston, Mass. 1987) is a more recent overview of Kant's life and work. Anthony Storr's book, *Solitude* (Fontana, London 1989) contains an intriguing section on the psychological motivations of Kant's writing.

Books by Kant

The heart of Kant's philosophy lies in the three *Critiques*. The most frequently consulted translations in English of the *Critique of Pure Reason* and the *Critique of Practical Reason* are by Norman Kemp Smith (Macmillan, London 1978; a different edition edited by Norman Kemp Smith is published by St Martin's Press, New York 1969) and Lewis White Beck (Maxwell Macmillan International, Oxford 1993 & Macmillan, New York 1993) respectively. James Creed Meredith's translation of the *Critique of Judgement* is widely used (Oxford University Press, Oxford & New York 1973), although a very good translation by Werner S. Pluhar has recently appeared (Hackett Publishing Company, Indianapolis 1987). This book also contains a useful introduction by Pluhar to Kant's critical philosophy.

Kant's writing is notoriously dense and complex, albeit engrossing. Readers may be pleased to know that Kant issued two shorter versions of the first two *Critiques*. *Prolegomena To Any Future Metaphysics That Will be Able to Come Forward as Science* (ed. P. Carus, tr. J.W. Ellington, Hackett Publishing Company, Indianapolis 1996) was published shortly after the *Critique of Pure Reason* in 1783; it provides a useful overview of the first *Critique* whilst asking how it is possible for science to establish the conditions of its own possibility. *Groundwork of the Metaphysics of Morals* (tr. H.J. Paton, Routledge, London & New York 1995) was published in 1785, three years before the second *Critique*, and offers an initial sketch of Kant's main themes in his critical practical philosophy, including an outline of the concepts of duty, free will and the categorical imperative.

A complete edition of Kant's collected writings does not exist yet in English, although Cambridge University Press is at present engaged in completing such an edition (*Cambridge Edition of the Works of Immanuel Kant*), and many of Kant's works, including many of his pre-critical writings, are already available through this edition.

Introductions to Kant

Many writings on Kant tend to be complex and esoteric. However, a few introductions to his thought have been published, such as R. Scruton's *Kant* (Oxford University Press, Oxford 1982). Histories of Western philosophy also always contain a section on Kant (see for example *The Oxford Illustrated History of Western Philosophy*, ed. A. Kenny, Oxford University Press, Oxford & New York 1994).

Other important works on Kant include G. Deleuze's *Kant's Critical Philosophy* (tr. H. Tomlinson and B. Habberjam, Athlone Press, London 1984). This is a short but dense book by a philosopher in his own right which highlights the sense of interaction between the three *Critiques*. H. Caygill's *A Kant Dictionary*, Blackwell, Oxford & Cambridge, Mass. 1995 is a highly comprehensive and helpful genealogy of Kant's philosophical concepts. For a revaluation of Kant in terms of feminist thought, see L. Irigaray's article, "Sexual Difference" (in *French Feminist Thought: A Reader*, ed. T. Moi, Blackwell, Oxford & Cambridge, Mass. 1993). *The Blackwell Companion to the Enlightenment* (ed. J.W. Yolton, Blackwell, Oxford & Cambridge, Mass. 1995) is useful for providing a sense of the historical and philosophical context to Kant's work.

Readers interested in further introductions to philosophy are advised to consult other titles in the *Introducing* series.

Author's acknowledgements

I would like to thank Catherine Yass and Meg Errington for their generous help and support throughout the preparation and writing of this book. I am grateful also to Juliet Steyn and Richard Appignanesi for their interest and kind advice.

I would like to dedicate this book to my Mother and Father, Jean and Ernest Want.

Artist's acknowledgements

The artist wishes to thank Dom Klimowski, Natalia Klimowska, Joe McDonald and Danusia Schejbal for their invaluable help in designing the book.

Christopher Want is an Art Historian and Philosopher. He teaches Art Criticism and Theory at Kent Institute of Art and Design, and Critical Theory at Goldsmiths' College. He has published widely on Romantic and Postmodern art and philosophy.

Andrzej Klimowski is an award-winning designer and illustrator, the author of the acclaimed graphic novel *The Depository*, and a lecturer at the Royal College of Art. He has also illustrated introductory guides to Picasso and Walter Benjamin in this series.

Typesetting by **Wayzgoose**

Index